THE CHILD'S BOOK
ON THE SOUL

Thank you for your
dedication and service
To Christis Kingdom
and Covenant Church.

Jon Burton
Clerk of Session

2007

THE CHILD'S BOOK
ON
THE SOUL

Two Parts in One

PART FIRST.

Thomas H. Gallaudet

Solid Ground Christian Books
Birmingham, Alabama USA

Solid Ground Christian Books
PO Box 660132
Vestavia Hills, AL 35266
205-443-0311
sgcb@charter.net
http://solid-ground-books.com

The Child's Book on the Soul

Thomas H. Gallaudet (1787-1851)

Taken from 1836 edition by The American Tract Society, NY

Solid Ground Classic Reprints

First printing of new edition September 2007

Cover work by Borgo Design, Tuscaloosa, AL
Contact them at **borgogirl@bellsouth.net**

Cover image is taken from an engraving in the original edition

ISBN: 1-59925-116-7

PREFACE

A Few Important Words for Parents or Teachers

_____

To teach a child, that he has something within him, distinct from the body; unlike it; wonderfully superior to it; and which will survive it after death, and live forever; is the simple, elementary principle of all religious instruction.

This, too, is one of the first truths of religion, if not the very first, which the child is best able to comprehend, and which excites in him the deepest and most abiding interest in this momentous subject.

He perceives the objects which are addressed to his senses. He sees his own body, and can easily be made to notice and understand many of its peculiar qualities. He can be led to observe, that some of these qualities are like those belonging to the various, material objects around him.

He is conscious of his own sensations, emotions, and states of mind. It is wonderful, at how early an age he can be led to notice, and discriminate between them. In fact, he does this, every time that he says he is *hungry* or *thirsty, glad,* or *sorry;* every time that he says, *he knows, he thinks, he believes, he remembers, he forgets;* every time that he understands you when you tell him, that he is *a good or a bad boy.*

Now, it is no very difficult task, to lead him to notice, that *material objects* give no evidence that they feel, or think, or act voluntarily. *But he does.* He is conscious of doing so. He has *something,* then, within him, which such objects have not. What is this something? Is it like the body, or wholly unlike it?

His body has qualities like those of the material objects around him. His body is *matter*. This something within him has no properties in common with matter. We have good reason, then, to conclude that it is wholly unlike matter. We call it *immaterial*. We give it a distinctive name, although we know nothing of its essence. We tell the child that he has *a soul*, meaning by this nothing more than that he has *something* within him which thinks, and feels, and recognizes the difference between right and wrong, and is entirely unlike his body, and distinct from it. He is told, that *his body* will die, and be laid in the grave and turn to dust; but that *his soul* will never die, that it is immortal.

Now he begins to feel an intense interest in the subject. Where will his soul be after death? Who will take care of it? How will it act; how will it feel?

He is then prepared to be taught, that there is *a Great Spirit*, like his own spirit, but infinitely superior to it, who made him, soul and body; to whom he is accountable; and who will reward and punish him after death, according as he conducts himself well or ill in this life.

Thus the foundation is laid for his arriving at the knowledge of the fact, that *God has made a Revelation to man*, and for his being taught the truths which this Revelation contains.

He may inquire, whether brutes have souls. Let him be answered candidly. They seem to have something within them which thinks, and is somewhat like the thinking principle in man; but it is immensely inferior to it; it is apparently incapable of distinguishing between right and wrong; and, with regard to its existence after death, we know nothing.

There are two important reasons, why a child should early be taught to notice, and discriminate between, its sensations, emotions, states, and operations of mind.

To do this, makes the child acquainted with its own spirit. The power of reflection is produced; consciousness is called into exercise; habits of self-examination are formed. The little thinker begins, already, to aspire to the dignity of *an intelligent being*. His conceptions on intellectual subjects, though limited, are sufficiently accurate for all the purposes of the present development of his mind and heart. With the aid of these conceptions, he forms his notions, and the only precise ones of which he is, as yet, susceptible, of the ETERNAL MIND.

For let it never be forgotten by all concerned in the religious instruction of youth, that *the elements of all our notions of the Father of our spirits, must be derived from what we know of the emotions, states, and operations of our own spirits. Without these elements, all that Revelation proposes to teach us of God, would be wholly unintelligible.*

Another reason why a child should be early led, according to the measure of his capacity, to become an Intellectual Philosopher, is, that, in no other way, can he form distinct conceptions of the meaning of those names and terms in our language which denote intellectual objects. If he has not noticed the states of his mind when he *remembers*, and when he *forgets*, and also discriminated between them, how can he possibly know the meaning of these terms?

The author of this little volume has endeavored, in writing it, to accomplish some of the objects which have been alluded to in the above remarks. He commits it into the hands of mothers, and of all who feel an interest, or take a part, in the religious instruction of children. He would recommend, that it should be read, at suitable intervals of time, to quite young children, rather than put into their hands. For those a little older it will serve as a reading book; though they should be examined with regard to their knowledge of its contents, and their comprehension of its reasonings.

If inquires are made, or difficulties started, or doubts expressed, by the child, let them be treated with the greatest attention. *They who would teach children well, must first learn a great deal from them.*

One simple truth, *that a child has a soul, distinct from the body, which will survive it, and live forever,* is the leading idea that is attempted to be illustrated and enforced. If the author has succeeded in doing this, let it not be objected, that he has not gone further. For one, he thinks, there is a great deal too much complexity in the early, religious instruction of children. They cannot learn every thing at once. Teach a child the truth contained in this book. Answer his inquiries concerning it. Elicit his own views and illustrations. They will often surprise you. Fix *this truth* in his memory. Engrave it upon his heart. Make him feel that he is not a mere animal; that he has other and higher enjoyments than those which are sensual; that he is an intellectual, moral, and accountable being, destined to an endless existence beyond the grave; and you have laid a foundation for teaching him that there is *a God, in whose hands is his eternal destiny; and that there is a Book, in which he can learn all that it is important for him to know with regard to the will of God, and his own happiness and duty.*

In conclusion, the author would beg leave to suggest, whether this volume might not be profitably used in the religious instruction of the lower classes of pupils in Sunday Schools; in Primary Schools, as a text book, for the teacher; and as a reading book.

Let the pupil read and have explained to him *one dialogue thoroughly.* Then propose the questions. It will test his knowledge of the subject. It will lead him to pursue continuous trains of thought, and teach him to *think for himself.*

———

PART I

———

A LETTER

To little Boys and Girls, from one who hopes they will learn, both how to *be good*, and to *do good*. For, *to be good, and to do good, is the only way to be happy.*

My Dear Children,

I have seven children. They often ask me to tell them stories; and I am glad to do so when they are good children, and do what their father and mother wish to have them do. I wrote this book for them, and they have all read it. I think it did them good to read it, and to learn from it some things which it was very useful for them to understand, even when they were quite young.

I thought it might do other little boys and girls good to read this book, or to have it read to them. So I have had it printed; and I hope, my dear children, that it will do *you good*, to learn and understand what I have written. If you cannot read it easily, you can get somebody to read it to you, and to tell you the meaning of any hard words which you do not understand.

I shall tell you a story about a little boy and his mother. The mother will say a great many things to the little boy, and he will say a great many things to his mother.

If you should sit down with any body; with your father, or mother, or brother, or sister, and talk with them for some time, you say many things to them, and they say many things to you, to do so, would be called *a dialogue*.

There will be several dialogues in this book. I did not write them only to amuse you, as your playthings do. I wish to do something more than to amuse you. I wish to teach you some things which you ought to know, and to remember, if you wish to be good boys and girls.

The mother we will call Mrs. Stanhope; and the little boy, her son, we will call Robert.

I do not know that there ever were such persons as Mrs. Stanhope and Robert. But I can tell you better what I wish to tell you, if I talk about a mother and her son, and if I give them both names. All that they say will be right, and it will do you good to know it, and you must try to understand, and to remember it.

Do not be in a hurry to get to the end of the story. Be attentive to every part of it. If you should not understand any word, or any thing which Mrs. Stanhope and Robert say to each other, be sure to ask somebody to explain it to you. This is the way you should always do, when you find any thing hard in the books which you read. It will not do you any good to read books, if you do not understand them.

And when your father or mother, or anybody, is talking with you, and you do not know what they mean, tell them you do not understand them, and ask them to please to explain it to you. And when they try to explain anything to you, or to tell you the meaning of any hard words, and you do not still quite understand them, do not be afraid to tell them so. *It is very wrong to say that you understand a thing, when you do not.*

Try to understand every thing you are reading or learning, or that anybody says to you, and then you will improve fast; and then you will become wise, and, I hope, also good and happy.

But I suppose you would like to hear the story about Mrs. Stanhope and her son Robert, which, I hope, will be both instructive and entertaining to you.

I am your friend,

THOMAS H. GALLAUDET

DIALOGUE I.

Robert Stanhope was five years old. His father died when Robert was a little boy. His mother had one other child, Eliza, who was three years old.

They lived in a pleasant town, in a small white house, near the church and the school-house.

Robert and Eliza did not go to school. Their mother said, they should go when they were a little older. She used to teach them at home. She was a very kind mother, and they both loved her very much.

Behind Mrs. Stanhope's house there was a beautiful garden. One day she was walking in it with Robert. He picked some pretty flowers, to give to his little sister who was in the house, and tied them together with a string which he had in his pocket.

After they had walked some time, they sat down on a seat, under a large, shady tree. It was in the afternoon, just before sunset. They breathed the pure, refreshing air. They smelled the sweet flowers which grew around them. They listened to the songs of the birds and the branches over their heads. All was calm and pleasant.

Robert had been a good boy, and he felt very happy. Mrs. Stanhope felt happy too. It always made her happy to see Robert a good boy. She took hold of his hand and kissed him. She thought she would talk a little with him, and teach him some good things. So she began.

Mother. Look, Robert. See that pretty, round, light stone. Pick it up, and hand it to me.

Robert. Here it is, mother. It looks like sugar. I would almost think it good to eat.

M. No, my son, it is too hard to eat. It would break your teeth if you should try to eat it.

R. What is it called, mother?

M. It is called a pebble, and I wish to talk to you about it. - If you should ask it anything, would it answer you?

R. No, mother; a stone cannot speak.

M. If you should try to teach it, could it learn anything?

R. No, no, mother; you know it could not.

M. Look at that beautiful rose in the nosegay which you have picked for Eliza. It is very different from the pebble. It has a stem and green leaves. It has soft, red and white leaves; and all put together, so as to make a very pretty flower. When it was on the rose-bush, it lived and it grew. And it will live a day or two longer, if Eliza puts it into a tumbler, and fills it with water. The rose is much more curious than the pebble. It *lives*, but the pebble does not. Talk to the rose, and see if it will answer you.

R. Mother, it will do no good for me to talk to the rose. Roses cannot hear or speak.

M. Can a rose be taught anything?

13

R. No, mother, no more than a pebble can.

M. Do you know who gave me this watch?

R. You told me that father did. What a pretty watch it is. Do open it, and let me see what is inside of it.

(Mrs. Stanhope opens the watch.)

M.   Look, Robert, and see how many curious, little wheels there are, that keep going round and round.

R. I see them, mother. I wish I had a watch that would go. Do you remember, the other day, when you opened your watch, and showed it to Eliza, she thought it was alive?

M. Yes, my son, but your sister is a very little girl, and did not know any better. *You* know, that the watch is not alive.

R. But it seems as if it was. It moves of itself.

M.   No, Robert, a watch cannot move of itself, any more than a rose, or a pebble can. It must be wound up with a key, and there is a spring inside which makes all the wheels go.

R. Mother, the watch, I think, is a great deal more curious than the pebble or the rose.

M. Well, see, then, if the watch will say anything to you, or if you can teach it anything.

R. It cannot speak, mother; and I cannot teach it, any more than I can the pebble or the rose.

M. Why cannot the watch speak, or learn any thing?

R. Oh! Mother, I have just thought why it cannot, and why the pebble and the rose cannot.

M. Well, what is the reason?

R. They have no mouths to speak with, and no ears to hear with.

M. Is that all the reason?

R. I do not know any other; if there is, will you please to tell me.

M. My son, it is beginning to grow dark. Let us go into the house, and, after tea, I will talk with you more about these things.

———

So they went into the house, and Robert gave his sister all the pretty flowers that he had picked for her. Eliza kissed her brother, and thanked him for the flowers, and put them into a tumbler, and filled it with water.

———

QUESTIONS ON DIALOGUE I.

Can a stone speak, or learn any thing?
Can a lump of earth? Can a piece of iron?
Tell me some *other things*, like stone and iron, that cannot speak, or learn any thing.
How is a rose different from a pebble?

What *other things*, besides a rose, live and grow?
Can a rose speak, or learn any thing?
Can a pink? Can a tulip? Tell me some *other things*, like a rose, that cannot speak, or learn any thing.
What is inside of a watch?
Is a watch alive? Does it move of itself? What is there inside of a watch, that makes the wheels go?
What must be done, to make a watch go?
Which is the most curious, the watch, or the rose?
Can a watch speak, or learn any thing? Tell me some *other things*, that are curious, like a watch.
Can *they* speak, or learn any thing? Tell me some *other curious things*, that cannot speak, or learn any thing. Why cannot the pebble, the rose, and the watch, speak?

DIALOGUE II.

After tea, Mrs. Stanhope told Eliza she might play a little while with her wooden blocks, and build houses on the floor. She then took her sewing and sat down by a table, and Robert sat down by her, in his little chair. He wished to have his mother talk to him again about the pebble, the rose, and the watch. He had kept the pebble in his pocket, and now took it out and laid it on the table. Mrs. Stanhope put her watch too on the table, so that she might see, when it was time for the children to go to bed. Robert began the conversation.

  Robert. While we were talking in the garden, mother, about the pebble, and the watch, you said you would talk more with me about them, after tea. Will you please to tell me the reason why they cannot speak or learn. I thought the reason was, because they have no mouths nor ears.

The Child's Book on the Soul

Mother. That is one reason, my son, but it is not all. A dog has a mouth, and lips, and teeth, and a tongue, very much like yours, but he cannot speak, nor learn to read.

R. But our dog Tray can make a noise. He barks very loud sometimes.

M. Can Tray say any words?

R. No, mother, not one. I wonder why he cannot, if he has a mouth, and lips, and teeth, and a tongue so much like mine.

M. Did you ever try to teach Tray to read?

R. No, mother, dogs cannot learn to read. But I have taught Tray to drive the ducks away from the yard in front of the house. And I have taught him to run after my ball and bring it to me, when I throw it away out into the road. But I wonder why he cannot learn to read. He seems to know many things.

M. He knows some things, Robert. But how many more things you and Eliza know, than poor Tray does. You and Eliza, too, can learn a great many *more* things, and *keep on learning* as long as you live, and read a great many books, and get a great deal of knowledge. But Tray cannot do so. He knows about as much now as he ever will know.

R. Mother, did Tray know, it was wicked to steal the meat out of the cellar when you whipped him for doing it?

M. No, he did not. He does not know any thing about what is right or wrong.

17

R. Do any dogs, or cats, or horses, or cows, or sheep, know any thing about what is right and wrong, mother?

M. No, my son, they do not. Men, and women, and boys, and girls, know what is right and wrong; but beasts, and birds, and fishes do not.

R. Do flies, mother?

M. No, nor any kind of insects; nor frogs, nor toads, nor worms, nor snakes. You see how very different you are, Robert, from all these animals, and from a watch, a rose, and a pebble. You can understand me, when I speak to you. You can speak to me, so that I know exactly what you mean. You can learn to read, and to write, and to do a great many different things, and you can keep on learning, and studying books, and getting knowledge. You know what right and wrong is. You feel happy, when you do right, and you feel unhappy, when you do wrong. Do you understand all this?

R. I think I do, mother.

M. Remember then, how very different you are from a pebble, a rose, a watch, and your dog, Tray. We will try, by and by, to find out, *what it is that makes you so different from them.*

R. Mother, do tell me now.

M. No, my son, I shall have to explain some things to you first, before you can understand me. Perhaps, in a few days, I shall be able to tell you about it.

R. Well, mother, I always find, you know best how to teach me, so I will wait till you are ready. But will you talk to me again soon, about the pebble, the rose, the watch, and Tray? I love to hear about them very much.

M. If you are a good boy, I will talk to you about them, tomorrow. It is time for you and Eliza to go to bed now.

QUESTIONS ON DIALOGUE II.

Can any thing that has no mouth, and no ears, speak, or learn any thing?

Can a dog speak? He has a mouth, and lips, and teeth, and tongue.

Can a horse? Can a cow? Can a sheep?

What *other animals* are there, which have a mouth, and lips, and teeth, and tongue, that cannot speak?

Can a dog make any noise? Tell me of some *other animals*, that can make a noise, but cannot speak.

Can a dog learn to read?

Can a horse? Can a cow? Can a sheep? Tell me of some *other animals*, that cannot learn to read.

What can you teach a dog? What a horse? What any other animals?

What things do *you* know, that a *dog* does not know?

What things can *you* learn, that a *dog* cannot learn?

What things can you *keep on* learning?

Can a dog *keep on* learning? *How much* can he keep on learning? Do dogs know, that it is wicked to steal?

Do dogs know any thing about what is right, and what is wrong?

What *other animals* are there, that do not know any thing about what is right, and what is wrong?

How are *you* different from beasts, and birds, and fishes, and insects?

How do you feel, when you do right?

How do you feel, when you do wrong?

Are you *very different*, from a pebble, a rose, a watch and a dog?

What *other things and animals* are you very different from?

Do you wish to know *what* it is, that makes you so different from them?

Do little children know best, how they should be taught? *Who* does know best?

―――――――――
―――――――――

DIALOGUE III.

The next day, soon after breakfast, Mrs. Stanhope and her two children went to take a walk in the garden. It was a fine morning. There was not a cloud to be seen, and the sun shone bright and pleasant. Their little dog Tray went with them, running and playing by their side. Eliza asked her mother, if she might go and pick some fresh flowers, to put into her tumbler with those which Robert gave her. Mrs. Stanhope said yes, and away ran Eliza, as fast as she could go, with Tray running after her. Mrs. Stanhope and Robert, after they had done walking, sat down on a bench, and talked with each other.

――――

Robert. Mother, you remember, you promised to tell me something more about the pebble, the rose, the watch, and my little dog. Only see, how he is running after Eliza.

Mother. I remember my promise, that I would do so, if you were a good boy. You have behaved very well, and we will talk a little before we go into the house.

R. I have been thinking this morning, mother, about what you told me last evening. And I thought, how very different sister Eliza is from the pebble. She is not like it at all.

M. But, Robert, is not Eliza like the pebble a very little?

R. How, mother, I do not understand you?

M. Can you lift the pebble?

R. Yes, mother, it is very light.

M. Can you lift Eliza?

R. Yes, I did the other day, but I could hardly do it, she is so heavy. Mother, she is heavier than I am. Mr. Smith weighed us, last Saturday afternoon, in his great scales.

M. Then Eliza has more weight than you. If Mr. Smith should weigh Eliza and the pebble, which would have the most weight?

R. Eliza would weigh as much as a great many pebbles.

M. Then she would have a great deal more weight than one pebble?

R. Yes, mother.

21

M. Then the pebble has something that Eliza has; for *they both have weight.*

R. That is true, mother, and I now see that Eliza and the pebble are a little alike.

M. Which feels the hardest, the pebble or Eliza's hand?

R. The pebble, mother; but Eliza's hand is pretty hard too.

M. Then Eliza and the pebble *both have hardness.*

R. Yes, mother, I see again, that they are a little alike.

M. See, Robert, Eliza is standing near the fence. Do you see her shadow on the fence?

R. Yes, mother. How exactly it is like her. If I had my slate and pencil here, I think I could draw that shadow.

M. Here is a lead pencil and some paper. See if you can draw it.

R. I will try.

Robert takes the pencil and paper, and draws the shadow.

M. You have done it very well. What you have drawn is the shape or form of Eliza. Now draw the form of the pebble.

Robert draws the form of the pebble.

R. Mother, the form of the pebble is round, but the form of Eliza is – I do not know what to call it – it is not round or square, but it is like her shadow.

M. Eliza and the pebble, then, *both have shape or form.*

R. Yes, mother, and this makes three things in which they are a little alike.

M. What is the color of the pebble?

R. White, mother. Oh! I guess what you are going to tell me now, that Eliza and the pebble *both have color.* But she has a great deal the prettiest color. She has a great many different colors. Her hair and her eyes are black. Her neck and her hands are white. Her teeth are white too, and what a beautiful red cheek she has. Mother, is she not a very pretty girl?

M. I hope your sister will be a *good* girl; for it is much better to be a good child, even if one is ever so ugly, than to be a bad child and ever so pretty.

Now tell me, Robert, in how many things Eliza and the pebble are alike.

R. They are somewhat alike in four things, mother; in *weight,* - in *hardness,* - in *form,* - and in *color.*

M. Suppose a lion should catch Eliza, and take her into his great mouth; could he not break her body into a great many pieces?

R. Mother, are there any lions near here?

M. No, my son, you need not be afraid of the lions. They live a great way from here, and can never hurt you nor Eliza.

R. I am very glad of that, mother.

M. If you should take a hammer and break the pebble, what would you break it into?

R. Into pieces.

M. Yes, my son, or you would break it into parts. It means the same thing.

R. And, I suppose, if a lion should catch my poor sister, he would break her body into a thousand pieces or parts.

M. Then Eliza and the pebble *both have parts.*

R. Yes, mother, but Eliza has a great many more parts than the pebble.

M. Come Eliza. Come Robert. It is time to go into the house and begin our little school.

So they went into the house, and Mrs. Stanhope sat down with them in the parlor, and taught them how to read and spell.

QUESTIONS ON DIALOGUE III.

Are you like a pebble *at all?*
Does a pebble weigh any thing? How much do *you* weigh?
Which has most weight, you or a pebble?
Tell me *some other things*, like a pebble, that have *weight*, as you have.
Has a pebble hardness? What *other things* have hardness?
Have *you* hardness? What *part* of you has hardness?
Is any part of you as hard as a pebble?
Tell me some other things, like a pebble, that have *hardness*, as you have.
Did you ever see the shadow of any little boy or girl?
Can you draw the shadow of a little boy? If you were to draw his
shadow, would it be exactly like him, as a picture is?
What do you mean by the *form* of a little boy?
Can you draw the form of a horse? Would it be like *your* form? Can
you draw the form of a pebble? Tell me some *other things*, like a pebble,
that have *form*, as you have?
You have weight and form, like a pebble; what *other things* have you, like
a pebble?
Tell me some *other things*, like a pebble, that have *color*, as you have?
If you were to break a pebble, *what* would you break it into?
If you were to be caught by a lion, what would he break *you* into?
Tell me some other things, like a pebble, that have *parts*, as you have.

_____
_____

DIALOGUE IV.

After Mrs. Stanhope had kept school one hour, she told Robert and Eliza they might play a little while. Eliza got her wagon, and put her doll in it, and went out into the front yard to draw it about. But Robert did not go to play. He wished very much to talk with his mother again, and asked her, if she would please to tell him something more about the pebble. She consented, and Robert stood by her side, for he said he was tired of sitting.

_____

Mother. Tell me, Robert, in how many things your sister and the pebble are alike.

Robert. I think I remember, mother. They are alike in having *weight, hardness, shape* or *form, color,* and *parts.*

M. Look, Robert, the rose that you gave Eliza is still alive. It has hardly faded at all.

R. She has poured some fresh water into the tumbler, mother, two or three times, and I suppose that has kept it alive.

M. Robert, try if you can tell me, in how many things the rose and your little sister are alike.

R. I can tell you, mother, some things in which Eliza and the rose are alike, because in some things they are both like the pebble.

M. Well, tell me.

R. Eliza, and the rose, and the pebble too, have weight, hardness, form, color, and parts.

M. That is right, my son; but which is most like Eliza, - the pebble, or the rose?

R. The rose, mother.

M. Why?

R. Because its shape is more like Eliza's shape; and it has several different, beautiful colors, like Eliza; and it has many parts, and so has Eliza.

M. Very well. But there is one other thing, my son, in which the rose is still more like Eliza. Can you think what it is?

R. I do not know, mother, unless it is, that *the rose grows.* For it was once a little bud, and it has grown to be a large flower.

M. You are right, Robert. Eliza was once a little infant, like the bud, and she will grow and be a woman, like the full-blown rose. *Eliza and the rose both have life.*

R. Mother, is Eliza's life like the life of a rose?

M. No, they are very different. The rose cannot feel, if you should break off one of its leaves. But Eliza can feel; and it hurts her, if you only pull one hair out of her head. The rose cannot go from one place to another; but Eliza can walk, and run about.

R. Is the life of a rose like the life of a pink, mother?

M. Yes, and it is like the life of all other flowers, and like the life of trees, and wheat, and rye, and corn, and potatoes, and turnips, and grass.

R. Mother, I remember you told me, one day, that all these things are called *vegetables*.

M. Yes, and their life is called *vegetable life*.

R. Mother, Tray feels when you hurt him, and he can go from one place to another. Is not his life like Eliza's life?

M. Yes, my son, and so is the life of all dogs, and cats, and horses, and cows, and sheep, and of all things that can breathe and move about. Their life is like the life of men, and women and children, and we call this *animal life*.

R. Then *my life* is not vegetable life; it is *animal life*.

M. You are right, my son. But we have talked long enough. Go and play a little while with Eliza, and then I will call you both to say another lesson.

_____

QUESTIONS ON DIALOGUE IV.

In how many things are you like a pebble?
In how many things are you like a rose?
Which is *most* like you, a pebble, or a rose?
In what thing are *you* like a rose, but *the pebble* is not?
Tell me some *other things*, like a rose, which have *smell*, as you have?
Does a rose grow?
What was it, when it was very small?
What were *you*, when you were very small?
Have you grown much? Do you grow any *now*?
Tell me some *other things*, like a rose, that *live and grow*, as you do. Is *your* life like the life of *a rose*?
Can a rose feel? Can *you*? Can a rose walk? Can *you*?
Tell me some *other things* that *cannot* feel or walk.
Tell me some *other things* that *can* feel and walk.
What are flowers, trees, wheat, rye, corn, potatoes, and grass, called?
What is their *life* called?
Can a dog feel? Can he go from one place to another?
Is a dog's life like *your* life? What do you call all things, that can breathe and move about?
What is your life, and the life of all things that can breathe can move about, called?
Is *your* life *vegetable life*?

30

————————

————————

DIALOGUE V.

In the evening Eliza was very tired, she had played so much, and she grew very sleepy soon after tea. Mrs. Stanhope went with her up stairs and put her to bed. She brought the candle down; for Eliza was a good girl, and always went to sleep, alone in the dark, without a candle.

Mrs. Stanhope then went into her library where she kept her books, and took Robert with her, and asked him if he did not wish to look at some pictures, but he said he would rather talk with his mother. So they sat down on a sofa, and Mrs. Stanhope began.

Mother. See, my son, if you can remember in how many things Eliza and the rose are alike.

Robert. I will try if I can, mother. The rose is like Eliza, in having *weight; hardness; form; color; parts;* and *life.*

M. What is the difference between Eliza's life, and the life of the rose?

R. Eliza has *animal life*, but the rose has *vegetable life.*

M. Now let us see, Robert, in how many things Eliza and the watch are alike.

R. I think I can tell, mother.

31

M. Well, try.

R.   They are alike, mother, in having *weight*, *hardness*, *form*, *color*, and *parts*.

M. Has the watch nothing else like Eliza?

R. I want to think a little, mother.

M.   That is right, my son; when you have a hard question to answer, always take time to think.

(Robert thinks for two or three minutes, and then says,)

R. Mother, I wish I could look inside of Eliza.

M. Well, what if you could?

R. I think, I should see some little wheels going round and round, like those in the watch.

M. What makes you think so, Robert?

R.   Mother, you know the little things on the watch, that you showed me, the other day. Let me look at them now.

M. Here, take the watch.

R. Mother, what do you call these two little things that go round and round, and tell us what o'clock it is?

M. They are called *hands*.

R. That is strange, mother; I was going to call them so, and to tell you, that the little wheels inside make them go, just as *something inside of Eliza, which makes her hands go.*

M. We must try to find what *this something* is, inside of Eliza, that makes her hands go.

R. That we can never do, mother.

M. Why not, my son?

R. Oh! Mother, you could not open my little sister, and look inside of her, without killing her.

M. That we will never do. But, do you remember the little boy who died, last winter, in the house, just beyond the bridge, and that I took you to see the corpse, before it was buried?

R. Yes, mother, and I never before felt as I did while I was looking at that little boy. I touched his cheek, and it was as cold as ice. I took hold of his little hand, but it was stiff. He had stopped breathing. He could not see, nor hear, nor move. Could he feel any, mother?

M. No, my son, no more than a pebble can.

R. William Baker was a pretty little boy, mother; I used to play with him a great many times. I am very sorry that he is dead. Why did they put him down into that dark hole in the ground?

M. I will tell you about that some other time, my son. Before he was buried, the physicians opened his little body, to see if they could find out what it was that made him die.

R. When I die, will *my body* be opened, mother?

M. I do not know, my son. Sometimes the physicians wish to open the body of a dead person, so that they may find out what made him die, and learn how to cure other sick persons.

R. I suppose, when they open a dead body, they can see all the little wheels inside, that made it go when it was alive.

M. Yes, my son, and when you grow older, you can learn all about what is inside of the body. But there are no little wheels inside of the body, like those in a watch. There are a great many different parts, however, that move one another, and make the whole body move. Do you know what it is that makes the wheels inside of a watch go?

R. Did you not tell me, mother, that it was a spring, and that it must be wound up, to make the watch go?

M. Yes, my son, the watch cannot make itself go, and if it were not wound up, it would soon stop going, and be still, and the hands would not move.

R. Mother, can any body make any thing that will go of itself, and keep going?

M. No, my son, I have never heard of any body that could. But what is it that makes Eliza's hands go?

34

R. Mother, some of those parts inside move one another, and then move her hands, just as the wheels inside of a watch move one another, and then move the hands of the watch. Is it not so?

M. I will talk with you again, about this, tomorrow, Robert. It is time for you to go to bed now.

QUESTIONS ON DIALOGUE V.

In how many things are you and a pebble alike?
In how many things are you and a rose alike?
What is the difference between *your* life, and the life of *a rose?*
What is the difference between the life of a potato, and the life of a horse?
Tell me some things that have animal life.
Tell me some things that have vegetable life.
In how many things are you and a watch alike?
What are those two little things on the watch called, that go round and round, and tell us what o'clock it is?
What makes them go round and round?
Have you any thing inside of you, that makes your hands go?
Do you think, that you have any *little wheels* inside of you?
What is it, inside of a watch, that makes the wheels go?
What must you do to the spring, to make a watch go?
Can a watch make itself go?
Why does a watch stop going?
Can any body make any thing, that will go of itself, and keep going?
Tell me of any thing *else*, that has wheels inside, and goes as a watch goes.
Tell me of any thing *else*, that can make itself move, as *you* can.

DIALOGUE VI.

The next day Mrs. Stanhope called Robert and Eliza very early, to go and take a walk with her before breakfast. The sun was just rising, as they left the house. The dew drops glittered on the grass. The birds sang sweetly. Every thing was pleasant, and Robert and Eliza, being good children, felt happy, and their mother felt happy in seeing them so. After they had walked about a mile, Eliza said she felt tired, and they all sat down on a large stone, to rest. Mrs. Stanhope took a book full of pictures from her work bag, and gave it to Eliza to look at. Then she and Robert had the following conversation.

Robert. Mother, you said you would talk with me today, about the watch and Eliza again.

Mother. We were trying, my son, to find out what is inside of Eliza, that makes her hands go.

R. Yes, and I thought it must be the parts inside of her, which move one another, and then move her hands, just as the wheels inside of a watch do.

M. But, the wheels inside of a watch would not go, if the spring did not set them a going.

R. Mother, has Eliza a spring inside of her too, that keeps her a going?

36

M. That is what we must try to find out. If she has, it cannot be like the spring of a watch, for that is made of steel, and Eliza has nothing like steel inside of her.

R. Yes, mother, and the spring of a watch has to be wound up every day, or it would not make the wheels go. And I am sure nobody winds up Eliza.

M. Robert, put your right hand to your right ear.

R. There, mother, I have.

M. Now put your right hand to your left ear.

R. I have, mother; - but why do you wish to have me do so?

M. Wait a little, and I will tell you. Now put your left hand to your left ear.

R. There it goes, mother.

M. Now put your left hand to your right ear.

R. I have – how quick it goes, mother.

M. What made it go?

R. It went of itself, mother.

M. Could little William Baker's hand go of itself to his ear, when he was dead?

R. No, mother.

M. Why not, Robert?

R. Mother, his hand was dead and stiff, it could not move, but mine is alive and limber, and so it can move.

M. What is the reason that your hand does not move now?

R. I do not wish to have it move, mother.

M. If you should wish to have your right hand go to your nose, would it go?

R. Yes, mother, there it goes just as quick as I think to have it go.

M. Think to have both of your hands go forward.

R. There they go.

M. Think to have them go backward.

R. There they go.

M. Could little William Baker think to have his hands go?

R. He could when he was alive, mother, - he used to make them go, a good many times, when he played ball with me. But when he was dead, he could not think any thing at all. *He could not think to have his hands go.*

M. Can a watch think to have its hands go?

R. Mother, a watch cannot think about any thing at all. It never thinks, and when it is not wound up, stops going, and it is just like dead William.

M. After a watch has stopped, and it is wound up again, will it go?

R. Yes, mother.

M. Can a watch wind itself up?

R. No, mother, you have to wind it up, or the spring would not make the wheels go.

M. How do I wind it up?

R. With your hand.

M. What makes my hand wind it up?

R. You think to have your hand wind the watch up.

M. Look here, Robert, my watch has stopped; the spring and the wheels do not move. Take it, and wind it up.

R. I am afraid I shall break it, mother.

M. I will show you.

(Mrs. Stanhope shows Robert how to wind the watch up, which he does very well.)

R. Mother, the watch goes again.

M. Yes, because you wound it up. What did you wind it up with?

R. With the key.

M. What made the key wind it up?

R. My hand.

M. Did your hand go of itself?

R. No, mother, I thought to have it go, and it went just as I wished to have it, and turned the key round.

M. Can you make your foot go, when you think to have it go?

R. Yes, mother, there it goes up.

M. Can you think to have any other parts of your body move?

R. Oh! Yes, mother, a great many. I can stand up, and sit down, and walk, and run, and hop, and jump, and throw my ball, and draw my wagon, and shake my head, when I want to say yes or no, and open my eyes and shut them, and open my mouth and shut it, and eat, and drink, and do, - Oh! A great many things whenever I wish.

M. Well, children, it is time for us to go back again. Give me the book, Eliza; you have been a good girl to look at it while Robert and I have been talking. Let us go home, and get some breakfast.

———

_____

QUESTIONS ON DIALOGUE VI.

Have you any thing, inside of you, like the spring of a watch, which makes your body move?

Put your right hand on the top of your head.

Put your left hand on the top of your head.

Put your right hand to your left eye.

Put your left hand to your right eye.

What made your hands go so?

Did you ever see a dead person?

Can a dead person's hand move? Why not?

Why does not your foot move *now*?

If you should wish to have your foot move, would it move?

Think, to have your hands go to your head.

Can a dead person *think*, to have *his* hands, or any part of his body, move?

Could a dead person, *before he died*, think, to have his hands move?

Can a watch think, to have its hands move?

After a watch has stopped, what must be done before it will go again?

Can a watch wind itself up?

How does a person wind a watch up?

What makes his hand wind the watch up?

Wind this watch up. Does it go? Why does it go?

What did you wind the watch up with?

What made the key wind it up?

Did your hand go of itself?

Think, to make some parts of your body move.

Can you think, to have any other parts move?

————————————
————————————

DIALOGUE VII.

There was a summer-house in Mrs. Stanhope's garden, which was covered all over with a beautiful honey-suckle. It was a shady, pleasant place, and cool, because the sun could not shine into it. There were seats inside of it, and Mrs. Stanhope often used to sit there with her little children.

After dinner, Robert and his mother went to the summer-house, and sat down on the bench, and Robert said to his mother:

Robert. Mother, will you talk with me again about the watch, and tell me what it is, inside of Eliza and me, that is so different from what is inside of the watch?

Mother. Yes, my son; you remember that the watch cannot go, unless the spring is wound up; and that the spring cannot wind itself up; and that somebody must wind it up with a key.

R. Yes, mother, and I am very different from the watch, because I can think to have my hands and feet go, and to do a great many things, and the watch cannot think to have its hands move at all.

M. Shut your eyes, Robert, cover them with your hand, and sit quite still; do not move your body, nor head, nor arms, nor feet.

R. Mother, I cannot sit so long, or I shall be very tired.

M. You need not sit so only a few minutes.

R. Well, I will try, mother.

M. Think of something *round*.

R. I have, mother.

M. What is it?

R. A ball.

M. What kind of a ball?

R. The little ivory ball that Eliza plays with, sometimes.

M. What color is it?

R. Red, and there is a string tied to it; and it looks just as if I could see Eliza playing with it, on her little stool, in the parlor.

M. You may open your eyes, Robert. Can you see Eliza, now, playing with her ivory ball?

R. No, mother, but I can, if I shut my eyes again. Oh! How many things I see when I am asleep, mother; I dreamed, last night, that I saw William Baker. He looked just as he did when he was alive. He ran very fast, and I tried to catch him, but I could not, and he ran away across the bridge, and I was a little frightened, and I awoke.

M. Were you in bed when you awoke?

R. Yes, mother, I had not moved at all; for I remember I went to sleep on my right side, and I was on my right side when I awoke.

M. I suppose, you could shut your eyes, and think you see William Baker, now.

R. Yes, mother, I do, and I see him just as I saw him in my dream.

M. You can dream that you run, then; or you can shut your eyes, and think that you are running, when your body is quite still?

R. Yes, mother.

M. You can *think that you are doing things, then, when you are not doing them?*

R. Yes, mother, I can think now, that I am driving my hoop all around the yard, while I am sitting here in the summer-house.

M. And you can *think that you are seeing things, when you are not seeing them?*

R. Yes, mother, I can think now, that I am looking at the beautiful picture, in your library, over the fire place.

M. Robert, how does a rose smell?

R. It smells sweet.

M. Does an onion smell like a rose?

44

R. No, mother, but very different. I do not like the smell of an onion.

M. How do you know? You are not smelling a rose and an onion.

R But I can think how they smell; and I can think how a great many other things smell.

M. Then, you can *think that you are smelling things, when you are not smelling them?*

R. Yes, mother, and sometimes when I have a bad cold, and cannot smell at all, still I can think how things smell.

M. And suppose you were lame, could you think that you were running?

R. I believe I could, mother.

M. And suppose you were blind, could you think of seeing things?

R. Yes, mother, I believe I could.

M. Which do you like best, a peach, or an apple?

R. A peach; it tastes a great deal the sweetest.

M. But you are not tasting a peach, or an apple.

R. No, mother, but I can think how they taste.

M. You can *think, then, that you are tasting things, when you are not tasting them?*

R. Yes, mother.

M. Which do you like to hear best, a flute, or a drum?

R. A flute, mother; and I can think, now, that I am hearing Uncle John play on his flute.

M. Then, you can *think that you are hearing things, when you are not hearing them?*

R. Yes, mother, and so I can *think that I am feeling things, when I am not feeling them.* I can think how a stone feels, and how my ball feels, and how your hand feels.

M. And can you think how *you feel,* when you are cold?

R. Yes, mother, and how I feel when I am warm, and when I am hungry, and when I am dry, and when I am sick.

M. Robert, is not all this very strange?

R. Mother, I wonder I never thought about it before. What is it that I have, which is so different from any thing that the watch has, or the rose, or the pebble? What is it: what do you call it, mother?

M. I am not quite ready to tell you yet. And it is best, now, for you to go and play a little. We have talked long enough.

46

QUESTIONS ON DIALOGUE VII

How are *you* different from a watch? *Its* hands move, and *your* hands
move. Does the watch move differently from what *you* do?
Put your hand over your eyes and shut them, so that you cannot see at
all. Think of something round. What is it?
Tell me all about it.
Open your eyes. Can you see it now?
What do you see, when you are asleep?
Do you ever dream of playing with any little children?
Do you ever dream of walking or running?
What *else* do you dream of doing?
Can you shut your eyes, now, and *think* of doing something, while you
are quite still?
What *other things* can you *think* of doing, while you are not doing them?
What things can you think of *seeing*, when you are not seeing them?
What things can you think of *smelling*, when you are not smelling them?
What things can you think of *tasting*, when you are not tasting them?
What things can you think of *hearing*, when you are not hearing them?
What things can you think of *feeling*, when you are not feeling them?
Can a pebble, a rose, or a watch, think so?
Have *you* something very different from any thing that a watch, a rose,
or a pebble, has?

DIALOGUE VIII

The next day was Sunday. Mrs. Stanhope went to church with
Robert and Eliza, who were good children, and behaved very
well. In the evening, after Eliza had gone to bed, Robert, who
was sitting at the table, looking at some pictures, asked his

mother to talk with him again about his *thinking*. She was glad to see him wish to improve. She shut up the book which she was reading, and said:

Mother. I wish to see, Robert, if you remember some of the things which I have taught you. Tell me, how you are different from a watch.

Robert. I can think to have my hands and feet move, and to do a great many things, - and then they do move, and I do the things just as I wish.

M. And how else are you different from a watch?

R. I can think, that I am doing things, when I am not doing them. I can think, that I am seeing things, when I am not seeing them; - that I am smelling things, when I am not smelling them; - that I am tasting things, when I am not tasting them; - that I am hearing things, when I am not hearing them; and that I am feeling things, when I am not feeling them.

M. Hold up your thumb, and look at it. Can your thumb think to do any thing?

R. No, mother.

M. Can your hand think to do any thing?

R. No, mother, it is *I* that think to have my hand move. My hand cannot think to have itself move. When I think to have it move, it moves just as I wish to have it.

M. Can your arm, or your foot, or any part of your body, think to do any thing?

48

R. No, mother, when they do any thing, they do it, because *I think first to have them do it.*

M. Shut your eyes, and think again about Eliza, playing with her ivory ball.

R. I do, mother, and I can think, how pretty she looks with her new, red frock on.

M. In what part of your body do you seem to be thinking, - in your foot?

R. No, mother, it seems as if I were thinking somewhere inside of my head.

M. Look at me, Robert, do you see me?

R. Yes, mother, I see you very well.

M. When William Baker was dead, did you see him?

R. Yes, mother, he was lying on a bed in the front room.

M. Was he just like *the William Baker* that used to play ball with you?

R. Yes, mother; only his face looked very pale, and his eyes were shut.

M. But William Baker, that used to play with you, could think to throw the ball and catch it, and do a great many things.

R. Yes, mother, and when he shut his eyes, I suppose he could think, that he saw a great many things which he did not see, just as I can.

49

*M. Then he had something inside of his head that could think –
just as you have?*

R. Yes, mother, but was that something inside of his
head, while he was lying on the bed when I saw him?

M. No, my son, it was not there. It was gone. If it had
been in his head, he could have thought to open his eyes, and
they would have opened; - he could have thought to speak to
you, and he would have spoken; - he could have thought to get
up, and he would have got up and played with you. You saw
William Baker's body, but it was a dead body, and the *something
which thinks* had gone out of it. It went out when he died.

R. It was only his dead body which I saw; *where had the
something that thinks, gone?*

M. That I will tell you some other time. But look at
me again, - do you see me?

R. Yes, mother, I have my eyes open, and see you very
well.

M. Suppose I should die, now, just as William Baker
did; would you see me then?

R. I would see your *dead body.*

M. Yes, my son, but would you see that something in
my head which thinks?

R. No, mother, and I cannot see it now. I wish I could
look inside of your head and see it. Or, I wish your head was
like glass, a little while, and then I could see it.

50

M. If you cannot see that something in my head which thinks, when you are looking at me, what is it that you see?

R. Mother, I see your *live body*, just as, when I was looking at William Baker, when he was lying on the bed, I saw his *dead body*.

M. *When you see a dead body, you know, that the something which thinks has gone out of it;* because the dead body cannot see, nor hear, nor smell, nor taste, nor feel, nor move, nor do any thing at all.

R. Yes, mother, and *when I see a live body, I know, that the something which thinks is still inside of it;* because it can see, and hear, and smell, and taste, and feel, and move, and do a great many things.

M. Well, my son, we have had a long talk, and I can see you begin to look a little tired. You may take the candle and go to bed now. Good night.

R. Good night, mother.

QUESTIONS ON DIALOGUE VIII.

How are you different from a watch?
What can you *think*, that you are doing, when you are not doing it?
Can your finger think to do any thing?
Can your thumb? Can your hand?
Who thinks to have your hand move, when it does move?
Can any part of your body think to do any thing?
Shut your eyes, and think of something.
In what part of your body do you seem to be thinking?

Look at me; do you *see* me?

When you look at a dead person, do you see *him*, just as you see *me*, now?

Have I something inside of *my* head, now, which thinks?

Has a *dead person* something inside of *his* head which thinks? Where has it gone?

When the dead body was alive, was there something inside of the head which could think?

If I should die now, would you see me then, just as you see me now? *What* would you see?

Can you see that *something* which is now inside of my head, and thinks? Look very attentively at me. If you do not see it, *what* do you see?

When you see a *dead body*, what do you know about the something which thinks?

When you see a *live body*, what do you know about the something which thinks?

———————————
———————————

DIALOGUE IX.

The next morning, Robert was up very early. His little sister had not yet risen, and he called Tray, and went and took a long walk.

When he returned, he went into the library, and took one of his books, and was reading it, when Mrs. Stanhope came in. He bade his mother good morning, and kissed her, and told her he had been taking a walk. Mrs. Stanhope said, that was right, and that it would make him strong and healthy. Then Robert asked his mother to talk with him again, about that something inside of our heads which thinks. She sat down, near the window, with him, and they began to talk together.

———————

Mother. Robert, what am I thinking about?

Robert. How can I know, mother, if you do not tell me? I cannot look inside of your head, and see your *thinking*.

M. Now, Robert, do you shut your eyes, and think about something.

R. Well, I do, mother.

M. If you do not tell me what you are thinking about, I cannot know. If you choose, you can keep all your thinking to yourself.

R. And so can you, and so can every body. William Baker, mother, sometimes used to say to me, "Give me a cent, and I will tell you what I am thinking about." And once Eliza talked in her sleep, so I suppose, I knew what she was dreaming about. Mother, *is dreaming and thinking, the same thing?*

M. They are very much alike. You know, when you dream, it seems to you as if you were awake.

R. Yes, mother, and I can see a great many things, which I cannot see when I am awake; and I can do a great many things, which I cannot do when I am awake.

M. Shut your eyes, and see if you cannot dream.

R. It is not exactly like a dream, mother, but it is almost, for I was thinking that I had wings and was flying.

M. Well, Robert, that something in your head which thinks, when you are awake, thinks too, when you are asleep; and *your thinking, when you are asleep*, is called *a dream.*

R. Mother, I dreamed once when I was awake.

M. What do you mean, Robert; how can that be?

R. Mother, I was sitting one day, in the parlor, looking into the fire, and seeing all the curious coals burn. It was almost dark, and there was no candle in the room. I kept looking and looking at the coals. At last, there was one coal that looked just like William Baker's face, and I began to think about him, and I thought we were playing ball together, behind the school house. And I kept thinking so a long time. At last, you came into the room, and spoke to me, and I turned round, and I did not seem to know where I was. It was just as I am, mother, when I wake up, out of a dream.

M. Your thinking all that time about William Baker, when you were so still, and looking into the fire, is called – *musing.*

R. One day, mother, I was looking over the bridge, and seeing the water run under it. And it kept running, and I kept looking at it. And I began to *muse* about sailing in a boat with William Baker. And it seemed as if we were sailing down the river. And at last we came near to the large rock below the bridge, you know, mother. And I was frightened, and began to think where I was. And I was so glad to find that I was not in the boat.

M. Yes, my son, then, also, you were *musing*.

R. What a curious thing that is which is inside of my head, mother. It thinks a great deal, and, while I am awake, it keeps thinking, always, about something or other.

M. Try, if you can stop thinking.

R. I cannot, mother; can *you?*

M. No, my son, I have been thinking ever since I was a little girl.

R. But not always, mother.

M. Why not, Robert?

R. Mother, you have been asleep a good deal of the time, and we do not always dream when we are asleep. Some nights I do not dream at all.

M. Well, I have thought a great deal, while I was awake.

R. So have I, mother. I do not think I could count all the different things that I have been thinking about. Oh! Mother, do tell me what that curious thing is, that is inside of my head, that keeps thinking so. You said you would.

M. I will, my son. Look at me. Be attentive, and never forget what I am going to tell you. That something inside of you which thinks, and keeps thinking, is your SOUL.

The Child's Book on the Soul

R. Oh! Mother, how glad I am that I have *a soul*, and that *you have a soul*, and that *little sister has a soul*. If we had not souls we could not talk with each other, and we could not love each other. Mother, is your soul, and Eliza's soul, like my soul?

M. This evening, Robert, I will tell you something more about the soul. It is time to go to breakfast now.

QUESTIONS ON DIALOGUE IX.

Look at me. What am I thinking about?
Can you look inside of my head, and see my thinking?
Shut your eyes, and think of something.
Can I tell what *you* have been thinking about, if you do not choose to tell me?
Can you keep all your thinking to yourself?
Is dreaming and thinking the same thing?
When you dream, how does it seem to you?
Can you dream *now*? What is dreaming?
What is musing? Did *you* ever muse?
Try to muse now. What have you been musing about?
Is not that a very curious thing inside of your head, that can do so many wonderful things?
Can you stop thinking? Try.
Have you *always* been thinking?
Can you tell me all the different things that you thought about yesterday?
Can you tell me all the different things that you *ever* thought about?
What is that *wonderful something* inside of you which thinks, and keeps thinking, called?
If we had not souls, could we talk with each other? Could we love each other?

———————————
———————————

DIALOGUE X.

In the evening, Robert put Mrs. Stanhope in mind, that she promised to talk with him again about the soul. She said she would do so, after Eliza had gone to bed; and she told Robert to sit down in his little chair, and study a short lesson, while she went up stairs with his sister. Robert was a good boy, and did as his mother bade him, and when she came down, she took a chair and sat by him, and they had the following conversation.

Mother. Robert, can you tell me what the soul is?

Robert. *My soul*, mother, *is that something inside of me which thinks.*

M. You have a body and a soul. I have a body and a soul. Eliza has a body and a soul. And every man, and woman, and boy, and girl, has a body and a soul.

R. Mother, have very little babies souls?

M. Yes, my son, but you know they do not think much, till they grow older.

R. Mother, does the soul grow?

M. Not like the body. But the soul is able to think more and more; and to understand more and more; and to

58

learn more and more; and to know more and more a great many good and useful things. And so we may say the soul grows.

R. But we do not give the soul food, mother, to make it grow, as we do the body.

M. No, my son. We cannot feed the soul, as we do a little child, when it is hungry. But we teach the soul a good many things. And this *teaching is the food of the soul.*

R. Mother, I wish you would teach me a great many things, so that my soul may grow fast, and be as large as uncle John's.

M. That I shall be glad to do, my son, and I hope you will make as good a man as your uncle John, too. But, tell me, Robert, is your soul any thing like a pebble, a rose or a watch?

R. No, mother, but *my body is;* because my body has weight; hardness; form; color; and parts; and so has a pebble, a rose, and a watch.

M. How many things can you see, Robert?

R. Mother, I cannot tell you how many things I can see. I can see almost every thing.

M. Can you see my soul, Robert?

R. No, mother, and you cannot see mine. I cannot see my own soul; but I can think how it thinks.

M. When you see things, what do you see?

R. I see how they look, mother. I see whether they are round or square; or long or short; or large or small; or red, or white, or black, or green, or yellow.

M. Then you see their form and their color.

R. Yes, mother, and I can see how far off they are.

M. You can hear a great many different things, making a great many different kinds of sound.

R. Yes, mother, I can hear the bell when it rings for church; and the stage-horn when the driver blows it; and the flute when uncle John plays on it; and the chickens, and the ducks, and the cow, and the sheep, and Eliza when she cries; oh! How many things I can hear!

M. Can you hear my soul, Robert?

R. I can hear *you*, when you speak, mother.

M. Yes, I think what I am going to say to you, and then, I think to have my tongue and my lips move; and I speak, and you hear the sound of my voice. Put your ear to this watch. Do you hear any thing?

R. Yes, mother, it goes, tick-tick, tick-tick.

M. Now put your ear close to my head. I am going to think. Try, if you can hear my thinking.

R. No, mother, I cannot at all.

The Child's Book on the Soul

M. My soul, then, makes no noise when it is thinking, and you cannot hear my soul, only you can hear my voice when I tell you what I am thinking.

R. That is very strange, mother. The soul must be very different from any thing that I can see or hear.

M. Yes, my son. And can you taste, or smell, or touch my soul?

R. No, mother, and I cannot taste, or smell, or touch my own soul.

M. You cannot tell, then, whether your soul is round or square, or long or short; or red or white, or black, or green, or yellow. You do not know that it has any form or color at all. You cannot tell, whether your soul sounds like a bell, or like a flute, or like any other thing.

You do not know that it has any sound at all.

You cannot tell whether your soul tastes like any thing.

You do not know that it has any taste at all.

You cannot tell whether your soul smells like any thing.

You do not know that it has any smell at all.

You cannot tell whether your soul is hard or soft, or whether it feels like any thing.

You do not know that it can be felt at all.

R. What do you call all those things, mother, that I can see, and hear, and taste, and smell, and touch?

M. We call them *matter*, and we say they are *material*.

R. Then my *body is material*.

M. Yes, my son, but your *soul is not material*. Or, what is the same thing, *your soul is immaterial*.

R. Mother, I suppose *your soul*, too, is immaterial; for I cannot see it, nor hear it, nor taste it, nor smell it, nor touch it.

M. Yes, every body's soul is immaterial. Remember, my son, that you have a body and a soul. Your body you can see, and hear, and taste, and smell, and touch. It is like the pebble, the rose, and the watch. *It is matter. It is material.* Your soul has not form, or color, or sound, or taste, or smell, or hardness, or softness. *It is not matter. It is immaterial*; or, what is the same thing, we call it *spirit*. The rose, the pebble, and the watch have no spirit.

But, you look a little sleepy. Go to bed, and tomorrow we will talk again about the soul.

QUESTIONS ON DIALOGUE X.

What is the soul?
Have all men, and women, and children, souls?
Does the soul grow? What is the food of the soul?
Do you wish to have *your* soul grow?
Is your soul any thing like a pebble, a rose, or a watch?
Tell me some *other things* that your soul is not like.

The Child's Book on the Soul

Is your *body* like a pebble, a rose, and a watch?
In what things is your body like a pebble, a rose, and a watch?
Can you see a great many things?
Can you see *my* soul? Can I see *yours?*
When you see things, of what shape or form are they?
When you see things, of what color are they?
When you see things, at what distance are they?
Can you hear a great many different things?
What things can you hear? Can you hear this watch?
I am thinking; can you hear my thinking?
Can you hear my soul, and tell me what kind of a *noise* it makes?
Can you tell how my soul *tastes?*
Can you tell how my soul *smells?*
Can you *touch* my soul?
Can you *see, hear, smell, taste,* or *touch, your own* soul, or any body's
soul?
Has the soul any form or color, at all? Has it any sound, at all?
Has it any taste, at all? Has it any smell, at all?
Does your soul fell like any thing? Can it be felt at all?
What do you call *those things*, that we can see, hear, taste, smell,
and touch?
Tell me *some things* that are matter.
Tell me some *more things*, that we call material.
What is your body?
Is your *soul* material? What is your soul?
What is matter? Is any body's soul material?
What is *every body's* soul?
How is your soul quite different from, and wholly unlike, your
body?
Your soul is not matter. It is immaterial.
What *else* do we call the soul?
What things have no spirit?

DIALOGUE XI.

The next morning Robert rose before sunrise. As he came down stairs, he met his mother. "Come, my son," said she, "let us go and take a walk in the garden. And, if you wish it, I will tell you something more about the soul." So they went into the garden, and while they were walking, they had the following conversation.

Robert. Mother, does not Tray think sometimes?

Mother. What makes you think so, Robert?

R. He stops, and seems to be thinking what he shall do, and then he runs away off, as if he meant to go after something that he had been thinking about.

M. Yes, and when you tell him, Robert, to go after your ball, you know he will go.

R. Mother, I have heard about a dog that used to carry a basket for his master to a butcher in the market, and get some meat, and bring it safely home. He used to do this very often, and the master would send the money by him, and write on a piece of paper and tell the butcher what kind of meat he wanted. I wish Tray could do so.

M. Well, I believe, Robert, that dogs think, and so do other animals. But that something within *them* which thinks, is very different from that something within *us* which thinks. *Tray has not a soul like yours.*

R. Mother, his *body* is a great deal like mine.

M. Yes, my son, he has animal-life, and so have you. He grows, and so do you. He eats, and drinks, and sleeps, and walks, and feels cold and warm, hungry and thirsty, sick and well, glad and sorry, and so do you. He will die, and so will you. His body will turn to dust, and so will yours. But, when you think of your soul, how different you are from Tray!

R. Yes, mother, and I am very different, too, from horses, and cows, and sheep, and birds, and fishes.

M. And from all things, Robert, that live and move, except men and women, and children. Their souls are like your soul, and we call the souls of men, and women, and children, *human souls.*

R. And, mother, do you call the bodies of men, and women, and children, *human bodies?*

M. Yes, my son.

R. Then, mother, I have a human soul, and a human body.

M. Yes, and there is one thing which makes you very different indeed, in your soul, from your dog Tray.

R. What is that, mother?

M. *You know what is right, and what is wrong, and he knows nothing about it.* You feel happy, when you think that you are a good boy; and unhappy, when you think that you are a bad boy; but Tray does not think and feel so.

Besides, you can talk, and he cannot. You can learn to read, and to write, and to cipher, and he cannot. As you grow older, you can study all the books in my library, and you can do business, like your uncle John; but Tray will never be able to do so. He will always be a poor ignorant dog as long as he lives.

R. Mother, Tray cannot laugh or cry.

M. No, my son, *his feelings are very different from yours.* You are pleased with looking at new pictures, and reading new books, and seeing new things, and having new thoughts, and getting knowledge, and thinking what you will do, when you grow up to be a man. Tray is not pleased with any of these things.

I hope, you feel the most happy, when you obey me, and think that you are a good boy, and are kind to Eliza, and to others, and try to do them good, and to make them happy. And, I hope, you intend, when you grow older, to do a great deal of good to others, and to make a great many people happy. Now, Tray does not have any thoughts or feelings like these.

R. I see, mother, more and more, how different I am from Tray.

The Child's Book on the Soul

M. Yes, my son, and if I had time I could tell you many other things in which you are very unlike your little dog. But I have said enough, I believe to show you that *the something inside of Tray which thinks, is very different, indeed, from your soul.*

R. Mother, has Tray any soul at all?

M. If he has a soul, Robert, it is not like a human soul. It is such a soul as beasts, and birds, and fishes have. I hardly think we ought to call it a soul.

R. What ought we to call it, mother?

M. I do not know, my son, exactly what to call it. It is *the something in beasts which thinks,* but there is no name for it.

R. Mother, uncle John told me, once, several stories about an elephant, and he said he thought elephants knew more than any other kind of beasts.

M. They seem to know a great deal, Robert.

R. Suppose, mother, you should take an elephant when he is very young, and have somebody to teach him all the time, could he ever learn so much as a man?

M. No, my son, if ever so much pains should be taken with him, till he was fifty years old, he would not know as much as your little sister does now. A little child, if he is well taught, will grow wiser and wiser, every day that he lives, and when he becomes a man, he will know more than all the elephants, and all the beasts in the world.

R. Mother, how much can a man learn?

M. I cannot tell you, Robert, - *your soul* can keep on learning and gaining knowledge as long as you live. You think *I* know a great deal, but there are some persons that know ten thousand, thousand times as much as I do.

R. Mother, I wish I knew *as much* as you do. I begin to think, how glad I ought to be, that I am so different from the beasts, and that I have a soul which can do so many wonderful things. If I were like Tray, I would feel very sorry. But, I have a soul, and I hope I shall be a wise and a good man.

I hope so, too, said Mrs. Stanhope; - and then they left the garden, and went into the house.

QUESTIONS ON DIALOGUE XI.

Does a dog, a horse, or cow, ever think?
Have you ever heard any curious story about a dog, or any other animal? Tell it to me.
Is that something inside *a beast*, which thinks, like the something inside of *us* which thinks?
Has a dog a soul like *yours*?
Has a dog a body like *yours*?
What has a dog like what *you* have; and what does he do, like what *you* do?
From what things that live and move, are you very different?
Whose soul is your soul like?
What kind of beings do we call men, and women, and children?
What kind of souls do we call the souls of men, of women, and of children?
What kind of bodies do we call the bodies of men, of women, and of children?

What is it, in *your soul*, that makes you very different, indeed, from a dog, and from all beasts?

How do you feel, when you think that you are a good boy?

How do you feel, when you think that you are a bad boy?

Has *a dog* any such thoughts or feelings?

You can talk. What *other things* can you do, that a *dog* cannot?

Will a dog ever learn more than he knows now?

Can a dog laugh or cry? What things delight *you*, which do not delight *a dog*?

What would it delight you *most* to do?

Has a dog any soul, at all? Have beasts, or birds, or fishes, or insects, human souls?

Have we any name for that something, inside of them, which thinks?

If an elephant should be taken, when he is very young, and taught all the while, could he ever learn as much as a man?

Can a little child, if he learns and keeps on learning, till he grows up to be a man, know more than all the elephants, and the beasts, in the world?

Can *you* keep on learning more and more?

Is not your soul, that can do all this, and keep on learning more and more always, a very wonderful thing?

Do you not wish to learn a great deal more about your soul?

DIALOGUE XII.

In the evening, Mrs. Stanhope once more took her seat by the table, and told Robert to come and sit by her. Eliza had gone to bed, a little while before. Robert seemed to be more and more glad to talk with his mother about his soul. And Mrs.

Stanhope was also happy to talk with him, he was so still and attentive to what she said.

———————

Mother. Robert, can you tell me what *matter* is?

Robert. Matter is any thing which I can see, hear, taste, smell, or touch.

M. What is *spirit?*

R. That something within me which thinks, and feels, and knows what is right, and what is wrong. It has not form, color, sound, taste, smell, hardness, or softness. You told me, mother, that it is the same as my *soul.*

M. You remember, Robert, we were talking, some days ago, about William Baker.

R. I remember it, mother.

M. You know, they put his body into a coffin, and carried it to the graveyard; and there they lowered it down into the grave, and covered it all over with earth.

R. Yes, mother, and I went the other day to see little William's grave. I love to go there and think about him, only it makes me cry, sometimes. The grass now has grown all over his grave, and there is a small white stone at one end of it, with his name on it, and it tells how old he was when he died.

M. When William Baker died, his body was put into the grave, but his soul was not. Your body, Robert, will be put into the grave, when you die, but your soul will not.

R. Will my soul live, mother, after my body is dead?

M. Robert, *your soul will never die.* Your body will die, and be laid in the grave, and turn to dust. But your soul will never die. It will live always.

R. I do not understand you, mother.

M. Look here, Robert; I will make as many marks on this slate as there are days in one year.

There, I have made the marks. Now, do you count them.

R. I have, mother, and there are three hundred and sixty-five.

M. That is right, there are three hundred and sixty-five days in one year. If I should make as many marks again, they all would be two years. Now, suppose I should fill all the slate full of marks on both sides, how many years, do you suppose, they all would make?

R. I do not know, mother. Perhaps they would make as many as ten years.

M. Well, they would, - about that. Now suppose, I should fill ten slates full, how many years would that make?

71

R. One hundred, mother, because ten tens make one hundred.

M. Suppose this room was full of slates, as full as it could be, one piled on the top of another, and every slate was full of marks, and every mark made one year; how many years would they all make?

R. Oh! I do now know, mother; I could not count them.

M. Suppose every room in this house was full of slates, all covered with marks; and every house in this town full of them, and you should carry them all into a large field, and pile them all, one on the top of another; - how many years would they all make?

R. Oh! Mother, nobody could tell. It would take you all your life to count them.

M. Well, my son, your soul will live as many years as all the marks, on all the slates, would make.

R. And will my soul die then, mother?

M. No, Robert, it will not die then. *It will keep on living.* It will live as many years again, as all the marks on the slates in the great pile. And then it will not die. It will keep on living. It will live as many years as all the marks would be on a hundred such piles of slates, - on a thousand such piles of slates, - on as many such piles as you can think of, from the ground away up to the sky, one on the top of another. And *then your soul will not die. It will still keep on living. Your soul will live for ever. It will never, never die.*

72

R. Oh! Mother, mother, how long my soul will live. I cannot think how long it will live. But where will it live? – where will it go to, when I die? Who will take care of my soul? What will it do? Will it keep thinking? Will your soul, and mine, and dear sister Eliza's go to the same place, mother, after we are all dead? Do you know? If you do, do tell me. I wish to know all about it, very much indeed.

M. Robert, I am afraid we have not time now. But it shall not be long before I will tell you about it. You will have a great deal to learn about your soul; and about where it is going to, after your body is dead and laid in the grave; and what you must do, that your soul may be happy for ever. For remember, *your soul will never die. Your soul will live for ever.*

Robert then went to bed; but he did not go to sleep for some time. He kept thinking about his soul, and wondering where it would go, after his body should die, and be laid in the grave.

QUESTIONS ON DIALOGUE XII.

What is matter? What is spirit?
Have you ever seen a person buried?
What was put into the grave?
Will *your body* ever be put into the grave?
Will *your soul* ever be put into the grave?
Will your soul live, after your body is dead?
Will your soul ever die?
How long will your soul live?

The Child's Book on the Soul

If you should cover a slate all over with marks, on both sides, and every mark should count one year; - will our soul live as many years, as all the marks would make?

If you should get a great pile of such slates, all covered with marks, reaching from the ground, away up to the sky; - will your soul live as many years, as all the marks, then, would make?

Would it still *keep on, and keep on,* living?

How many years will your soul live?

What do you mean by *for ever?*

Is it not wonderful that your soul will live for ever?

Do you not wish to know, *where* your soul will live, after the body is dead; *where* it will go to; and *who* will take care of it?

CONCLUSION TO PART ONE.

My Dear Children,

I have now finished what I meant to tell you about Mrs. Stanhope and her son Robert. I hope you have understood it all, and that you will remember it.

You see how much little Robert wished to have his mother teach him, so that he might get useful knowledge. And you, my dear children, should be very glad when your parents or elder brothers and sisters, or teachers, wish to talk with you about good things, and to make you understand what it is useful and important for you to know. Listen to them attentively. Remember what they say to you, and be thankful to them for all their kindness.

We should always try to get good from every book that we read. And can you not get some good from this little book? Will you not always remember, that each one of you, as well as little Robert, has *a soul*, which will live after the body is dead, and will live forever, - will *never, never, die!*

Think of this; ask your parents and teachers to tell you more about your soul; and what you must do, that your soul may be good and happy after your body is dead. Perhaps I, too, may tell you something more about your soul, in another little book like this.

I am your friend,

THOMAS H. GALLAUDET.

THE CHILD'S BOOK

ON

THE SOUL

Two Parts in One

PART SECOND

Thomas H. Gallaudet

Solid Ground Christian Books
Birmingham, Alabama USA

PREFACE

A Few Important Words for Parents or Teachers

———————

In the first part of the **Child's Book on the Soul**, the object was to illustrate and enforce one simple truth, *that a child has a soul distinct from the body, which will survive it and live for ever.*

In this continuation of that book, the inquiry of the child, whither his soul will go, after his body is dead, and who will take care of it, is attempted to be answered.

This answer leads to the consideration of some collateral topics, growing out of the main one, and intimately connected with it.

The two books contain instruction on the following subjects:

The immateriality and immorality of the Soul;

The existence of God;

His not having a body, but being a Spirit;

His omniscience;

His omnipresence;

His omnipotence;

His eternity;

His being the Creator, the Preserver, and the Governor, of all beings and things.

His goodness;

His holiness;

The fact, that He has given us a revelation of His will;

The leading principle of His moral government, that we must love and obey Him, and do good to others;

The sanctions of His moral government, in the rewards and punishments of a future state.

In all this, the proof of the existence of God, from the Light of Nature, and the Truth of the Sacred Scriptures, is not attempted. Perhaps, the author may yet do this. To bring the latter topic, however, down to the capacity of quite young children, would require a great deal of careful reflection, and of very patient analysis; if, indeed, the human mind, at five or six years of age, has attained to sufficient scope of thought, and power of generalization, to embrace it in its true and useful import.

Shall we forbear to teach children religious truth, and the truths of Revelation too, because, at an early age, they must, at first, receive and believe them, on the mere testimony of the parent? – Shall we hope to secure them against what some may call prejudice, by withholding from them this instruction?

If so, they must be removed from civilized society, and from all social intercourse.

Are there none but *religious prejudices*; none in business; in morals; in politics?

You wish your child to form his own opinions, without any bias, on all subjects that affect his eternal well-being. Let him not, then, feel the influences even of *your example.* If you treat the Bible, and the Sabbath, with neglect, your conduct speaks a louder language than words can do. *You predispose him to infidelity.* You give him a bias *against* Christianity. *You do not leave him entirely free to form is own opinions.*

It is idle, to think of training up a child, like a wild ass's colt, in such a freedom. Opinions he must form, and will begin to form, at a very early age. The parent is as much bound to furnish *his mind with useful truth, as his body with wholesome food.* In both cases, the child, if left to himself, may err, most sadly. And, in both cases, the parent must act conscientiously, according to his best judgment.

On the other hand, as the mind of the child strengthens, and his reasoning powers acquire sufficient maturity, he should never be discountenanced from inquiring into the evidences of those truths which he has been taught to receive on the authority of the parent. Let him understand the objections of the unbeliever in all their pretended force, and see by their fair refutation, and by the irresistible evidences of the truth of Revelation, both internal and external, that it rests on a basis which cannot be shaken.

When the consideration of these evidences, and a more faithful study of the Divine Oracles of Truth, shall form a part, and *a prominent part*, of the education of our children and youth, in this land, *called Christian*, then we may hope, and not till then, for a more general diffusion among us, not only of a speculative knowledge of what the religion of Jesus Christ is, but of the influence of its genuine spirit upon the hearts and lives of men.

Should the efforts of the author, in the humble task in which he is engaged, in any degree, contribute to the promotion of this great object, he shall feel, that he has not labored in vain.

It ought to be observed, that, although in the conversation between the mother and the child, in these books, there is a regular progression from one elementary, religious truth to another; still, the author would not, by this, mean to say that a child of five years of age may not be taught other important truths, and those which involve the peculiar doctrines of the gospel. For the sake of method, and it was necessary *to have some method*, he has taken a course of illustration which appeared to him to be the most simple and intelligible to the child.

An ample list of questions, for the benefit of the pupils in Sunday Schools, and in Infant Schools, will be found at the end of each dialogue.

They relate not only to the particular thoughts contained in the dialogues, but also to such other thoughts, as these would naturally suggest.

Let the pupil read, and have explained to him, *one dialogue thoroughly.* Then propose the questions. It will test his knowledge of the subject; it will lead him to pursue continuous trains of thought; and teach him to *think for himself.*

PART II

DIALOGUE I.

After Robert's mother had told him, that *his soul would never die*, he thought a great deal about it. Indeed, he lay awake a long time, that night, thinking about his soul, and wondering where it would go, after his body should die, and be laid in the grave.

The next morning, he rose very early, before any body in the house was up, and ran to his mother's chamber, and waked her, and asked her to talk with him, again, about his soul. Mrs. Stanhope told Robert, that he must be patient, and wait till breakfast was done, and that, then, she would do as he wished. He was a good boy, and went down stairs, and got his little book, and sat down to study his lesson. It rained very hard, that morning, so that he could not go out to take a walk. After breakfast, Mrs. Stanhope and the children went into the library, and while Eliza was amusing herself with looking at some pictures, Robert and his mother had the following dialogue.

Robert. I am astonished, mother, to think, that *my soul will never die*. I knew that my body would die. For I saw William Baker, after he was dead; and I thought, then, that I also should die, and that my body would be laid in the grave. I felt very much afraid to die.

Mother. Do you now feel afraid to die, my son?

R. Yes, mother, I do. I felt afraid to die *before*, because I thought I should be put down into the ground, and be covered all over with earth, and never see you, nor Eliza, nor any body else, any more.

But *now* I feel most afraid to die, because I do not know where my soul will go, or who will take care of it, after my body is dead, and laid in the grave.

M. That is what I will try to explain to you, and I hope to make you understand what you *must do*, so that you need not be afraid at all to die.

R. Oh! Mother, how glad I shall be, to know that. Why will you not tell me all about it *now*, before you begin to keep school?

M. You must have a little patience, Robert. Do you not remember, that you wanted to know, all at once, about your soul, *that something within you which thinks, and feels, and knows what is right and wrong?* You had to wait, then, till I could explain it to you, only as fast as you could understand me; and, after a while, you seemed to know pretty well all that I wished to teach you.

And now, I must talk to you, in the same way, slowly and carefully; or else you will not understand me.

R. Mother, I always find out, that you know best how to teach me. I will not be impatient; but only do begin.

M. When you die, your soul will immediately go out of your body. You wish to know, *where it will go, and who will take care of it.*

84

R. I do, mother; I do. For, suppose I should *die soon*, while I am a little boy, as William Baker did, I should leave you, and go away, - I do not know where, - and I should have no kind mother to take care of me! Who would take care of me?

M. Your Father, my son.

R. *My Father*, mother, is dead. I do not know where he has gone. Shall I go to the same place where he is, so that he can take care of me?

M. I hope you will, my son. But it is *another Father* that I mean.

R. Mother, I do not understand you. You used to tell me, that my father's name was like mine. You have shown me his name, on the tombstone, in the graveyard; and I wept, when I saw you weeping, while we stood near his grave. I do not remember him, but you have told me, that he was a very good man, and very kind to you and to me, and that you loved him very much. But who is my *other* father? Have you ever seen *him*? *Where* is he? I want to see *him*, too, very much.

M. Robert, you had a father who died when you were a little boy. He was the father of Eliza, too. He was my husband. His name was Robert Stanhope.

But you have *another Father*, who lives above that blue sky. He is the Father of *Eliza*, and of *me*, too, and of *all the men, and women, and children* in the world. If you are a good boy, and *do what He tells you to do*, you will go *where he is*, when you die, and He will take care of you, and make you happy forever.

R. Mother, did you ever *see this Father*?

M. No, my son, but I have *a Book* which tells me about Him, and what we must do to please Him; so that He will love us here, and love us when we die, and take up *our souls*, to live with Him forever, in that beautiful place where *He lives*.

R. Oh! Mother, what is the name of this good and kind Father: and what is the name of the place where he lives?

M. His name, my son, is GOD. He lives in *Heaven*. We call Him our Father, who is in Heaven, or *our Heavenly Father*.

R. My dear mother, how many new and wonderful things you have told me! I want to know a great deal more about God, my Heavenly Father; and about that beautiful place, called Heaven; and about that Book, which you have, and which tells you about these things.

M. My son, I am glad to see you so anxious to learn more of God. I hope to be able to teach you *out of that Book* which He has given me, and to teach you to study this Book yourself. For *it is the best of all books*. It makes those wise who read it; and those who love it, and obey it, need not fear to die. For it tells them that their souls will go to Heaven, as soon as their bodies are dead, and be happy in Heaven forever, where God, their Heavenly Father, will always love them and take care of them.

But we have talked a long while, and must stop now. You and Eliza may go out and play, for it does not rain, and when it is time, I will call you in, to school.

———————————

QUESTIONS ON DIALOGUE I.

Are you afraid to die? Why *not?* Or,
Why are you afraid to die?

Do you wish to know what you *must do,* so that you need not be afraid to die?

If you should die, *who* would take care of your soul?

Where do we read, and learn, about our Father who is in Heaven, and what we must do to please Him?

Where does He live, and where shall *we go,* if we do what He tells us to do?

What has God given us, to teach us about Himself?

Who are *those* that need not fear to die?

Who will always take care of them, and where will their souls go, as soon as their body is dead?

DIALOGUE II.

In the afternoon, Robert's aunt came to see Mrs. Stanhope; so that his mother did not talk with him, in the evening, about his soul. She promised, however, to do it, the next day, after his aunt had gone. His aunt was going to take Eliza home with her, to stay two or three weeks; and Robert felt a little sorry to have his sister go, and leave him. But he knew, that it would make Eliza happy, and do her good, for she was not quite well, and so, after bidding her, and his aunt, good-by, the next morning, he saw them ride away in the chaise, and went into the house with his mother.

Mrs. Stanhope told Robert, that she would take a walk with him, and go to the bank of the beautiful stream which was not far from their house. It was a place where she often walked. There was a shady grove of trees near the bank, and a seat under one of the trees; and there Robert and his mother sat down; and while all around them was pleasant and still, they talked together.

Robert. You promised, mother, to tell me more about God, my Heavenly Father; and now I shall be very glad to hear you.

Mother. Perhaps, my son, I may say some things which it will be difficult for you to understand. *God is so great, and we so little; He is so powerful, and we so weak; He is so wise, and we so ignorant; that we must not expect to know a great deal about Him.* Sometimes, you say, it is hard for you to understand things

which *I* say, and things which *I* do, because you are such a little boy; and I tell you, that you will understand them when you grow older. So, we can know but little of God, *now*. If we love and obey Him, we shall go to Heaven when we die, and *there* our souls will know more about God; and difficult things will be explained to us; and we shall keep on learning more and more about God, and his goodness, for ever and ever.

R. Mother, I do not wonder that it must be difficult to understand many things about God. I can hardly understand *how He is*, at all. Is He like us, mother?

M. In some things, we are a little *like Him*, Robert, but *He has no body. He is all Soul. He is a Spirit. He is the Great Spirit, who made you and me, and all the people that are in the world; and all the beasts, and birds, and fishes, and insects; and every thing that grows; and the earth; and the sun, and moon, and stars: and He takes care of every thing that He has made; and He governs all beings, and things.*

R. How *strong* God must be, mother, to do all this! But I cannot understand how it is, that He has no body. If He has no body, He has no eyes. How can He *see*, then, to take care of every thing?

M. I told you, my son, that there would be some things about God, which it would be difficult for you to understand; and this is one of those things, - how He can see to take care of every body and every thing, when *He has no eyes like ours*. But, perhaps, I can explain to you a *little* how this is. For I, myself, know but very little about it.

R. Do, mother, and I will be very attentive.

M. You remember, I taught you some days ago, how very different your soul is from your body. You can see, hear, taste, smell, and touch your body. *It is matter.* But your soul has no form, or color, or sound, or taste, or smell, or hardness, or softness. It is not matter. It is wholly unlike it. *It is spirit.*

R. All that I remember, mother, and I think, I understand it pretty well.

M. You remember, too, that you told me, that you could *think* you were seeing things, when you were not seeing them.

R. Yes, I remember that, too, mother.

M. Well, if the spirit is so very different from the body, it is not strange, that *it acts very differently from the body.* The body has eyes which see the things at which *they* look, *and the spirit has its eyes, too, which see the things at which they look.*

R. But I have no eyes, *inside of my head*, mother, where my spirit is.

M. It is true, my son, that your spirit has no *such eyes*, as those with which you are now looking at me. But *your spirit can see things in itself*, when your bodily eyes are shut; and so, because we cannot find any better word to use, we say the spirit has eyes. All that we mean is, that the spirit can see things in itself, and without the help of the bodily eyes.

R. I begin, mother, to understand you a little better; but still, I do not understand you very well.

M. What is this, Robert?

R. Your watch, mother.

M. Now, shut your eyes, and tell me whether my watch is a gold, or a silver one.

R. It is a gold one.

M. How do you know so? You do not *see* my watch.

R. But I can *think exactly how it looks.*

M. *You see it in your spirit, or in your mind.* You see it with *the eyes of your* mind; just as, when you look at the watch, you see it with your *bodily eyes.*

R. May I open my eyes, now, mother?

M. No, keep them shut a little longer.

R. It is very hard to do so.

M. I will tie my handkerchief round your head, Robert, and that will make it more easy for you to keep your eyes shut.

(Mrs. Stanhope proceeds to tie her handkerchief round Robert's head.)

R. Now, mother, I cannot see at all, even if I were to try.

M. Well, my son, tell me how your sister Eliza looks.

R. If she looks as she did this morning, mother, she looks a little pale. I think she was not very well, and, perhaps, too, she felt sorry that she was going to leave us.

M. But you do not *see* Eliza, and you could not see her, if your eyes were open.

R. But I can *think exactly how she looks*, mother.

M. Can you think exactly how William Baker looked, when he was alive?

R. Yes, mother, I can; I see him now, standing, just as he used to do, sometimes, at his father's door, when I went to play with him.

M. You see your little sister, then, who is *alive*, and your little playmate, who is *dead*, equally well, in your mind, or, as we may say, with the *eyes of your mind.*

Now, Robert, tell me, if you can think how our house and garden look.

R. I can, mother, and it seems as if I saw the road beyond our house, and the church, and the other houses.

M. Can you think of that beautiful prospect which I took you to see, when we went up the high hill, near your aunt's?

R. Oh! Yes, mother, I see it all, the fields, the woods, the river, the houses, the men at work, the cows, the sheep, and the beautiful water-fall, just as if I were standing now, on the top of that same hill.

M. Can you think of a great many persons and things, that you have seen a great while ago?

93

R. I can, mother, and I suppose if I were to keep thinking all day, with my eyes blindfolded, about things that I have seen, I could see *them all*, just as I have seen them before.

M. You saw them, before, with your *bodily eyes*. Now, you would see them *in your spirit*, or, as we may say, *with the eyes of your mind*.

If, then, you can see *in your spirit* so many, many persons and things, it is not difficult for the GREAT GOD to see, *in His Spirit*, or *with the eyes of His Mind*, all the persons and things which He has made, and which He takes care of.

As you can see things, although your bodily eyes are shut; so God can see things, although *He has no bodily eyes*. He sees all persons, and all things. He sees you at all times. *He has always seen you, and He will always see you. He sees all you think and feel, as well as all you do. You can hide nothing from Him.*

God does not love people who do wrong. Fear then, my son, to do wrong, or to say any thing wrong, or to feel wrong, or to think wrong. For remember, God *always sees you.*

R. Oh! Mother, *how great God is!* I hope I shall always *do*, and *say*, and *feel*, and *think* what is *right* so that God may love me, and take me up to Heaven when I die.

M. I hope so, indeed, my dear son. But it is growing late. Take off the handkerchief, and let us go home. This evening, I will talk with you again about God, your Heavenly Father.

QUESTIONS ON DIALOGUE II.

Can we expect to know a great deal about God? Why not?
Do you sometimes find it difficult, to understand what your parents say
and do? Why?
Shall we *ever* know more about God than we do now?
Is God like *us*?
Has God a body? Who is God?
What has God *made*, and what does He *do*?
What is *matter*? What is *spirit*?
Is your soul like your body?
What is your body? *What* is your soul?
Does the spirit act like the body?
Can you shut your eyes, and see things?
How do you see them? You do not see them with the eyes of the
body.
What do we mean, when we say, that the spirit has eyes?
When you shut your eyes, can you think exactly how things look?
Tell me, now, of *different things* that you can think of, how they look?
Can you think, now, of a great many persons and things that you have
seen, a great while ago?
How did you see them *before?*
How do you see them *now?*
How does God see all beings and things?
Has God always seen you?
Does He always see you?
Whom does God not love?
What should you fear? Why?

———————————
———————————

DIALOGUE III.

Mrs. Stanhope did not forget her promise, to teach Robert again about God, in the evening. She sat down with him by the window, in the parlor. They had no candle in the room. The moon shone so bright, that they needed no other light. The sky, too, was filled with stars. Robert, as he looked abroad on the scene, had feelings which he never had before. "How great God is," said he; "*how powerful He must be* to have made, and to take care of, that bright moon, and all those beautiful stars!"

M. Yes, my son, and God is *as good* as He is great. *He takes care of you, and of all little children, and of every little bird that builds its nest upon the trees.*

R. But, mother, when *you* take care of me, and of Eliza, you have *to be* where we are. When *you* take care of the different things in the house, you have *to go* about the house, from one room to the other. If God has no body, how can *He go* from one place to another, to take care of every thing, as He does?

M. God *is every where.* He is in all places, at all times.

R. Mother, it is very difficult for me to understand what you mean.

M. Robert, there are a great many things which we believe, and which we still find it very difficult to understand. —

96

Is not our spirit something very different from your body, and wholly unlike your body?

R. Yes, mother; I seem to understand that pretty well.

M. Where is your spirit, or soul?

R. Somewhere inside of my body, and it seems to me that it is in my head; for when I think hard, I seem *to feel the thinking in my head.*

M. How much room does your spirit take, in your head?

R. I do not know, mother; does it take any room at all?

M. If it is inside of your head, Robert, it would seem as if it must have *a place* there, if it is ever so small a place, and so take up *some room.* If your spirit takes up some room in your head, it would seem as if it must have some *length*, and some *breadth.* And, If your spirit has length and breadth, it is like *a pebble*, in one thing, for a pebble has length and breadth; and, if your spirit is like a pebble, *it is like matter.*

R. Well, mother, I see what a strange thing my spirit is. It must be inside of my head. And yet, as my spirit is not like matter at all, it is inside of my head, *I cannot tell how.*

M. My son, if *your spirit* is so strange a thing, and if there are some things about it which it is so difficult to understand, only think how much *more difficult* it must be, to understand many things about God, The Great Spirit.

The Book which He has given us, teaches us a great many things about Him, which we never should have learned in any other way. It is very kind in God, thus to teach us about Himself; and *we must believe all that he teaches us, although we can understand but little about it, and although some things may be hard to understand.*

R. I find as I grow older, that I begin to understand some things a great deal better than I once did, mother. I used to believe them, because *you told me so*, and I knew you always told me the truth. I could not think once, how it was, that a piece of iron could make a needle come to it, when the needle was some way off, and the iron did not touch it.

You told me about it, but it almost seemed to me, as if it could not be so, it was so difficult to understand *how* it could be so.

M. But when I showed you the piece of iron, (*or magnet,*) then you found out what I said was true.

R. Yes, mother, but though I saw the needle move to the magnet, with my own eyes, still I could not understand *how* it was done, and I do not know how *now*. Do you know, mother?

M. No, my son, I do not. And there a thousand things which I see, and know to be true, but which are very difficult to be understood.

God made all these things, and we must not wonder, then, if there are a great many things *about Him*, difficult to be understood.

R. Does He tell us, mother, in His Book, that He is in all places?

M. He does, my son. If He had a body, He would not be in all places, at the same time. He would have to move about from place to place, just as we do. But *He has no body. H is nothing but Spirit.* And there is some way, which we cannot understand or explain, in which he is in all places, and sees all things, and knows every body that has ever lived, or will ever live, and every thing that has ever happened, or will ever happen.

R. Mother, does God know *every single word* that you have ever said?

M. Yes, my son, and every thing that I have ever thought, or felt, or done. *He knows all that you have ever thought, or felt, or said, or done,* and all that every body that is in the world has thought, or felt, or said, or done. *There is not any thing which God does not know.*

R. Does God know, mother, every thing that is in all the books in you library?

M. Yes, my son, and every thing that is in all the books in the world. *God never has to learn any thing.* He does not have to wait, as you must, to see a thing happen, before He knows it. He knows whether it will rain tomorrow or not. He knows the very day, and hour, and minute, when you will die. He knows all the people that will live in the world, a hundred years hence, and a thousand years hence, and all their names, and all that they will do, and all that will happen to them.

R. Mother, *how little I know!*
M. Yes, my son, we are like little infants, or like the worms that crawl on the ground, when we think of God, and how great He is, and how much He knows. We should be very

glad, and very willing to have Him teach us out of *the Book* which He has given us, and be thankful that we can understand even a little of what is in it.

But it is time for you to go to bed. The moon shines so bright, you will not need a candle. Good night.

R. Good night, mother.

QUESTIONS ON DIALOGUE III.

Of *what* does God take care?

Does God go from one place to another, when he takes care of people and things?

Where is God?

Where is your spirit, or soul?

How much room does your spirit take?

If it takes up any room, what must it be like?

Can you tell, how your spirit is inside of your head?

Is it easy for you to understand every thing about your own spirit?

Can we expect to understand a great deal about God, the Great Spirit? Why not?

Where do we learn almost all that we know about God?

Suppose we find some things in the Book which God has given us, hard to be understood, what must we do?

Are there any things which you believed, when you were a little child, because your parents told you so, and which you have since found to be true? Tell me some *such things*.

Do you not see, and believe many things, to be true, although you cannot understand, or explain, *how* they are? Tell me some *such things*.

Ought we to believe every thing that God tells us? Why?

If God had a body could he be in all places?

Can we explain, *how* it is that God is in all places?

Can you explain how it is, that your soul, if it is not matter, is inside of you?

What does God know about you?

What does God know about every body?

What does God know about every thing?

How does God get his knowledge? Does he have to learn?

Does God know what *has* happened?

Does God know what *will* happen?

How much do you know?

How should we feel towards God, if He is willing to teach us?

DIALOGUE IV.

The next morning was a delightful one. The sun shone bright and clear, over the eastern hills. The air smelled sweet. Many happy birds were singing in the trees, and Robert, as he walked abroad with his mother, thought of the goodness of God, and admired the things which He had made.

Robert. You told me, mother, last evening, that *God is as good as He is great.* Will you please to tell me now *about his greatness?* For I wish to know more and more of God.

Mother. That I am glad to do, my son, but you will have, again, to be very attentive; for I must explain to you many things, before you can understand even a little about the *power of God.*

R. What is *power?*

M. That is the very thing that I was going first to explain to you. Look at that large stone. Do you think you can lift it up from the ground, and toss it over yonder fence?

R. I am afraid I cannot, but I will try.

(Robert takes the stone in his hands, and carries it to the fence, and tosses it over the fence, into the field.)

M. Well, you have done it; but it was heavy, was it not?

R. Yes, mother, but I determined I would toss it over the fence, if I could; and I held it as tight as I could, with my hands; and I strained my arms, and stood up straight, and tossed it *with all my might*, and over it wen. I should not like to try to do it again, for it has hurt my arms a little.

M. Take up that small pebble, and throw it over the fence.

R. There it goes, mother; I could have thrown it ten times as far.

M. When you threw the pebble, did you have to strain your arm any?

R. No, mother, hardly at all. I just raised my arm, and made it go forward, and opened my fingers, and away the pebble flew.

M. Raise your hand to your head.

R. There it goes.

M. Did you strain your arm any, then?

R. No, mother, not at all. I only *thought that my hand should go to my head,* and my whole arm moved, and my hand went to my head directly.

M. When you carried the large stone and tossed it over the fence, you felt strong, - *you felt that you could do it again,* if you should try, - di you not?

R. Yes, mother.

M. *You feel now, that you could do it again,* do you not?

R. I do.

M. You feel, then, that you are able to lift, and carry, and toss over the fence, *any other stone,* as heavy as that one.

R. Yes, mother, and I think, if I should try very hard, I should be able to toss one over that is a little heavier.

M. Your being *able to do so,* we call *power.* Have *I* power to toss a stone as heavy as the one you did, over the fence?

R. Oh! Yes, mother, you have the power to toss one over, five times as heave.

M. Then I have five times as much power as you have, to toss heavy stones over the fence.

R. Yes, mother, and I think uncle John, who is a man, and a good deal stronger than you are, has twenty times as much power as you have to lift, and carry stones, and toss them over the fence. I think he could lift that large rock from the ground; but I do not think he would have power to toss it over the fence.

M. Robert, when did you use the *most power*, - when you tossed the large stone over the fence, or when you threw the small pebble?

R. When I tossed the large stone. If I had used much power, when I threw the small pebble, it would have gone almost out of sight.

M. Not quite, Robert, but it would have gone a great deal farther than it did.

Did you use *any power*, when you raised your hand to your head?

R. I think I did, a little. I felt a little as I did when I was tossing the stone, and throwing the pebble.

M. Can you tell me, my son, some *other things* that you have *power to do?*

R. I have power to walk, and run, and jump; and to open my eyes and shut them; and to speak; and to look at things; and to take a great many different things into my hands, and do something with them.

M. If I should tie your feet with a string, Robert, would you have any power to run?

R. No, mother; but I should have power to take my knife out of my pocket, and cut the string in two, and run away.

M. Suppose I should command you not to do so, and go away and leave you alone; would you have power, then, to cut the string and run away?

R. Yes, mother, *I should have power to do it;* but I should not *wish* to do it, because I should be a naughty boy, to disobey you.

M. Robert, if you would have power to cut the string and disobey me, then you would have *power to be a naughty boy.*

R. Oh! Yes, *I feel that power,* sometimes, mother, when I do not like what you tell me to do; or when I wish to do what you tell me I must not do.

M. *You have power, then, to do wrong, and you have power to do right.* Do you see that this is so?

R. Yes, mother, I am sure of that; or else, you ought not to punish me when I do wrong, or reward me when I do right.

M. Has your dog Tray *any power* to carry a stone?

R. He can carry one in his mouth.

M. What other things has he power to do?

R. He can walk, and run, and jump, and do a great many things just as I do.

M. Then he has *one kind* of power like yours

But has Tray any power like yours, to do what is right, or what is wrong?

R.   He has not. *He cannot have, because he does not know what is right, or what is wrong.*

M.   Then you have, my son, a kind of power, which beasts and birds, and such other animals, have not.

If you have power to do what is right, or what is wrong, *be careful how you use this power.* God sees you at all times, and He knows whenever you use this power to do wrong, and He is displeased with every body that does wrong.

R.   I will try, mother, indeed I will, to do right at all times. Will God love me then?

M.   Yes, my son, for He loves all good people, and He will *love you*, now, as long as you live, and forever in Heaven, if you will *love and obey Him.*

R.   But, mother, you have not told me any thing yet about *the power of God.*

M.   You cannot understand any thing at all about *the power of God,* until you first understand something about *your own power.* That is the reason why I have been explaining it to you.

But we have got nearly home, and we must talk together again about *the power of God,* some time today, when it is convenient.

_____

QUESTIONS ON DIALOGUE IV.

What heavy thing can you lift, and carry, and throw?
What light thing can you throw?
Raise your hand to your head.
Do you feel, that you are able to lift, and carry, and throw some heavy things?
What do we call your *being able* to do so?
Have *I* more power than *you*? Why?
Has any person more power than *I* have?
Do you use more power at one time, than at another?
Did you use any power, when you raised your arm to your head?
What things have you power to do?
If I should blindfold you, and tell you not to take the handkerchief off, would you have power to do it?
Have you power to disobey your parents?
Have you power to do what is right, or what is wrong, just as you choose?
Would it be right for your parents to punish you for *not flying?* Why not?
Would it be right for your parents to punish you for not going on an errand, if they should tell you to go? Why?
Whould it be right for your parents to punish you for not teaching your little brother or sister, *to understand how to make a watch?* Why not?
Would it be right for your parents to punish you for not being kind to your little brother or sister? Why?
Would it be right for your parents to reward you for dreaming a beautiful dream? Why not?
Would it be right for your parents to reward you for learning a good lesson? Why?
Do you feel that you are naughty, because you do not know how to swim under water, like a fish does?
Should you feel that you were naughty, if you did not know your letters?

Why do you feel unhappy, when you do wrong?
Have *beasts* any power like yours?
Have beasts power to do what is right, or what is wrong? Why not?
How should you use your power to do what is right and what is wrong?
Whom does God love?

DIALOGUE V.

In the afternoon, Mrs. Stanhope heard Robert read, and say his lessons, in the summer-house, in the garden. After he was done, he said, he did not wish to go and play, but that he would rather stay and talk with his mother again about the power of God. She said she would do so, for a little while; and Robert, sitting by her side, and looking very attentively at her, was happy to learn something more of that good an great Being, our Father who is in Heaven.

Mother. Can you tell me, Robert, what *power* is?

Robert. Uncle John has a great deal *more power* than I have.

M. What do you mean by that?

R. I mean, that he is able to do a great many things that I am not able to do.

He has power to split a hard log of wood with an axe, and I have not. But I have power to do many things. You remember, I told you about them, this morning, mother.

M. Yes, my son, and as you grow older you will have *more power*, and will be able to do a great many things which you cannot do now.

R. Do you remember, mother, that you told me once about a very strong man, called Samson, who pulled a great house down, and killed a great many people who were in it?

M. Yes, my son, he was the strongest man that ever lived.

R. He must have had a great deal of power.

M. God, my son, has such great power, that *He can do all things*.

R. Could God pull the sun down, mother?

M. If God should *only think* to have the sun fall down, it would fall down just as quick as your hand went to your head, when *you thought* to have it go.

R. Would it be as easy for God to think to have the sun fall down, as it is for me to think to have my hand go to my head?

M. Yes; if God *should think* to have the sun, and moon, and stars, and the world, and all the people, and animals, and things, that are in it, destroyed, they would be destroyed, *just as easily and as soon*, as you can destroy a piece of paper, by throwing it into the fire.

R. Oh! Mother, I hope God will not do so.

M. God is as good, my son, as He is powerful. He always does what is right, and what is for the best good of all who love and obey Him.

R. You said, mother, that God can *do all things*. Can He make any thing that He chooses to make? Could he make *a new sun?*

M. Yes, and a mission if He chose, and a million of new moons, and worlds, and stars.

R. Mother, how did God make the sun?

M. *How* did you make your little box, the other day?

R. I made it out of paper.

M. *What* did you use, to make it?

R. I used your scissors.

M. And did you use *nothing else?*

R. I used my fingers, to be sure. I cannot make any thing without using *my hands.*

110

M. God took *nothing out of which* to make the sun; and he used *nothing with which* to make it.

R. I know, you have told me, that God has no body. Then He has no hands; but if He has no *hands*, I do not see how He can make any thing.

M. When you *think* to have your hand move to your head, it goes there. When God *thinks* to have any thing made, it is made. When there were no sun, nor moon, nor stars, God said, "Let there be light," and there was light.

R. How could He speak, mother, if He has *no mouth?*

M. If you could say *one word*, and immediately make a large tree spring up out of the ground, would you not think that you had great power?

R. Yes, mother, I should have more power than any body I now; I should have *power a good deal like God's.*

M. You would so, Robert. Well, when we wish to talk of the great power of God, we say, *He spoke, and it was done.* We mean, by this, that is as easy for him to *think*, and to have a thing immediately done, as it is for you or me, to speak.

The magnet has power *to draw* the needle. But we cannot tell what this power is. We say, *it draws the needle.* But we do not mean that it takes hold of the needle, as you do, when you take hold of any thing, to draw it to you, but only that its power is *something like this.*

So when we say, that God spoke and it was done, we mean that His power is *something like* what your power would

111

be, if you could, *by a word*, make a new, full grown tree spring up at once, out of the ground.

R. Oh! How much I must learn, mother, before I can understand even a little about God.

M. Yes, my son, we do indeed know, and understand, but little of the power of God.

God made all beings and things.

If he chose, He could destroy all beings and things, instantly. He can do any thing that He chooses. If all the people in the world should get together, and agree to try to keep God from doing any thing, they could not. All the power of all the people in the world is like dust, when we think of the power of God. He could destroy it, just as easily as you can blow a little dust away in to the air.

Nobody can think how great the power of God is.

God has all power.

GOD IS ALMIGHTY.

As God made all beings and things, and takes care of them, and does them good, *it is right that he should govern them.*

You know it is right that I should govern you and Eliza.

R. Yes, mother, you are very kind to us, and I know, that we should do what you tell us to do.

M. God, my son, knows all things. He knows *what it is right* for you to do, and *what it is best* for you to do – and what it is right *for every body* to do, and what it is best *for every body* to do.

If I did not govern you and Eliza; if I did not tell you what to do, and what not to do, we should have a great deal of trouble in our house. And if God did *not govern* the world, and all the people and things that are in it, and all the beings and things that He has made, - there would be trouble every where, - *there would be nothing but trouble, and confusion, and unhappiness.*

God is *good*, and he knows that it is *best* that he *should govern* all begins and things. He is *almighty*, and He *will govern* all beings and things. Those who *like Him* to govern them, and love and obey Him, He will love, and make them happy, forever. But those who *do not like Him* to govern them, and will not love and obey Him, He will not love, and make happy, forever.

R. Mother, *I begin to fear God*

M. You should *fear to displease Him*, my son, by doing any thing which He tell you not to do, or by neglecting to do what He commands you to do.

But if you love and obey Him, you need not fear Him, for He will take good care of you, and use his great power only to do what will be for your best good.

R. How will God use his power towards those who *will not love and obey Him?*

M. Do you not think, my son, that God will have to punish them: as I have to punish my children, when they are naughty and do not obey me?

R. Yes, mother, but *how* will God punish them?

M. He tells us, in the Book which He has given us, that they who do not love and obey Him cannot go to Heaven, to be happy with Him forever. Heaven is so good a place, all the people there are so good, and love God and love each other, that wicked people cannot go there. They *could not* be happy there themselves, and they would make all the others unhappy.

R. Where will the wicked people go, mother?

M. If they *keep on* being wicked; and will not feel sorry that they have been wicked; and tell God that they are sorry; and pray to Him to forgive them, and help them to become good; - and strive themselves *to be good and to do good*; - after they die, *their souls will go to a very unhappy place, called* Hell, where all the people are very wicked, and do not love God and each other, - and where God has told us, in the Book which He has given us, that those who will not love and obey Him, *shall go away into everlasting punishment.*

R. Oh! I hope I shall not go there, mother. I will try to love and obey God; so that I may go to heaven, when I die, and be good and happy forever.

M. May God, indeed, take you there, my dear son! But I shall have yet to teach you a good deal more about God, and what you *must do* to please Him.

Let us go into the house now.

QUESTIONS ON DIALOGUE V.

Can you tell me what *power* is?

How much power has God?

Would it be difficult for God to destroy all things?

Can God make any thing He chooses?

Out of what did God make the sun?

What did God use, to make the sun?

If God has *no hands*, how can He make any thing? What does God do first, before the thing is made?

What do we mean, when we say, that God spake, and it was done?

What do we mean, when we say, that the magnet *has power to draw the needle?*

Does it draw the needle, as you draw a thing to you, with your hands?

Can we understand much of the power of God?

What do you mean, when you say, that God is Almighty?

Is it right that your parents should *govern* you?

Why is it right that God should govern *all beings and things?*

If your *parents* were not to govern you, and the children, and the people that are in your house, what would happen?

If a *teacher* was not to govern his scholars, what would happen?

If the people that live in a town were not governed, what would happen?

If God was not to govern the beings and things which He has made, what would happen?

Whom will God make happy?

Whom will God not make happy?

How should you fear God?

If you love and obey God, how will He use his great power towards you?

How will God use his great power towards those who will not love and obey Him?

Where will their souls go to, after their bodies are dead?

_____

_____

DIALOGUE VI.

Mrs. Stanhope did not think of conversing with Robert, in the evening, about God. But he wished so much to learn a little more, before he went to bed, that his mother consented, and they had the following dialogue.

_____

Robert. I thought, as I was sitting alone, after dinner, mother, that I would ask you, how long God has lived.

Mother. My son, do you remember your little cousin Jane?

R. Oh! Yes, mother I have seen her twice, - once when she was a very little infant, - and again when she was about a year old.

M. Had she grown a good deal, the second time when you saw her?

R. Yes, she had; she was much larger and heavier.

M. Do you think she will keep on growing?

R. Yes, if she lives, she will keep on growing, till she gets to be a tall woman.

116

M. All the men and women in the world, Robert, have been little infants, and grew, and kept growing, till they grew up to be as tall as they now are.

R. I hope, mother, I shall grow to be as tall as uncle John is.

M. We cannot tell about that, Robert. You may die, long before you grow up to be a man.

But you asked me how long God has lived. I will tell you. *He* never was a little infant. He never grew. *He has always been as great, and as good, as He is now.*

R. Did he *always know* as much as He does now?

M. Yes, my on. He is very different from us. When you were a little infant, you knew hardly any thing. You began to understand a few things. You kept on learning more and more; and now you know a good many things, for such a little boy as you are.

But God never did so. His mind was never like that of a little infant. *He never had to learn,* so that he might understand different things.

He knows all things, and he has always known all things.

R. But, mother, does God know what happened before He was?

M. *Nothing happened,* my son, *before God was;* for no being lived before God, and there was nothing made before God, because, you know, He made all beings, and all things.

117

R. But *what was there before God was;* was there nothing at all, and nobody at all? Was it all empty and dark?

M. My son, *God has always lived.* There could not, then have been any beings, or any things, *before Him.*

R. Has nobody lived as long as God has?

M. God lived before all the men and women that ever lived. He lived before this world, and the sun, and moon, and stars, were made, long, long, long, before.

R. How long, mother, would it take me to count as many years as God has lived?

M. It is now eight o'clock. Let me see how many you can count in one minute.

(Mrs. Stanhope looks at her watch, and Robert counts till she tells him to stop.)

R. How many did I count, mother? I counted very fast.

M. You counted just one hundred. That would make *six thousand in one hour.*

God has lived a great deal longer than six thousand years. Now, if you were to keep on counting *two hours*, it would make *twelve thousand.* But God has lived a great many years longer than that.

R. Suppose I should keep on counting, mother, *all day and all night.* Would that make as many years as God has lived?

M. If you were to count so long, you would count *twenty-four hours,* and it would make *one hundred and forty-four thousand years.* But God has lived a great deal longer than that.

Now, if you could keep on counting, *as long as you live,* and you could put *it all together,* and know how many years it would make, it would only help you *to begin to think* how long God has lived. You would have to add *as many years again* to this, and *as many years again,* and *keep on* adding, and adding, and adding, and you would never come to the end. All this would only help you still, *to begin to think* how long God has lived.

God never began to live. He has always lived. No being ever helped Him to live, or takes any care of Him. *He* made all beings and things, and takes care of them. If *He* had not been, *they* never would have been.

As God never began to live, so He will never cease to live. *He will always live.* His being never had a beginning, and it will never have an end. *He is eternal.*

When you ask me how long God has lived, I answer;

GOD IS ETERNAL.

R. Mother, how wonderful! I am afraid that I shall never know much of God. *The more I think about Him, the less I seem to know.*

M. You know, my son, that your soul will never die. If you love and obey God, you will go to Heaven, and there you will keep on knowing more and more about Him, forever.

Let us think a little, and remember what you have learned, so far, about God.

God has no body. – GOD IS A SPIRIT.

He made all beings and things; and we say, GOD IS OUR CREATOR.

He takes care of all beings and things; and we say, GOD IS OUR PRESERVER.

He governs all begins and things; and we say, GOD IS OUR GOVERNOR.

He sees and knows all beings and things, that ever have been, that are now, or that ever will be; and we say, GOD IS OMNISCIENT.

He is in all places, at all times; and we say, GOD IS OMNIPRESENT.

He can do all things. He has all power; and we say, GOD IS OMNIPOTENT, or GOD IS ALMIGHTY.

He always was, He is, and He always will be; and we say, GOD IS ETERNAL.

Now, my son, you may go to bed. I have talked with your longer than I thought I should. Good night.

R. Good night, mother.

QUESTIONS ON DIALOGUE VI.

Were you ever smaller than you are *now?*
Have you grown much? Do you grow now?
Was God ever a little infant? Has *He* ever grown any?
Was He *ever* different from what He is *now?*
Did God ever have to lean any thing?
What happened before God was?
What was before God was?
Has any body, or thing, lived as long as God has?
If you were to keep on counting *all your life*, could you count as
many years as God has lived?
If you could count all the sands in the world, and count as many
again, and as many again, and as many again, and keep on counting,
would that ever be as many years as God has lived?
Did God ever *begin* to live?
Who made God? *Who* takes care of God?
How long will God live?
What do you mean, when you say, that God *is eternal?*
What do you mean, when you say, that God *is our Creator? Our
Preserver? Our Governor? That God is Omniscient? Omnipresent?
Omnipotent? Almighty? Eternal?*

_____

_____

DIALOGUE VII.

As Mrs. Stanhope and Robert were walking, the next morning, he said to her, "Mother, how I should like to go up that high hill yonder, and look all around, and see the beautiful country. Do you think that we could see aunt Mary's house from that hill?" "I believe we could, my son," said Mrs. Stanhope, "and if you do not feel tired, I am willing to walk longer, and go up the hill. There is a seat, under a shady tree, on the top of it, and we can sit down there, and rest ourselves, before we come back." "Oh! I am not tired at all," said Robert. And away he ran, and let down the bars of a fence through which they had to pass. When they had passed through, he was careful to put up the bars again, and he and his mother ascended the hill. After they had seated themselves, Robert began.

Robert. Mother, this is a good place for you to tell me something more about God.

Mother. Why do you think so?

R. It is so cool and pleasant. There is nothing here to disturb us. And then we can look all around, and see the many beautiful things that God has made.

M. I am glad to hear you say so, my son. Wherever we go, we see the things that God has made, and how kindly, too, He takes care of them. We see how good He is, in every pretty flower that grows, and in every little lamb that plays so happily by the side of its mother.

R. Mother, do you not think the bees are very happy? You remember you took me to see a bee-hive once. They are always flying about among the sweet flowers, and they have a great deal of sweet honey to eat.

M. Yes, my son, they are very happy; and one reason, I think, why they are so, is, that they are so busy and industrious. If you wish to be happy, you must be *industrious* too.

R. What did God make the bees, and sheep, and so many different kinds of animals for, mother?

M. He made them to show us his great power, and skill, and goodness; and He made a great many of them for our use and comfort. You know, that the stockings which you wear in the winter, and your clothes, too, are made from the wool that grows on the sheep's back.

R. Yes, mother, and I should be very cold if I did not wear them.

M. You would suffer a great deal, in winter, if you had not warm woolen clothes. Only think, then, how good God is, in making the wool to grow on the sheep's back, for your use and comfort.

R. And, mother, you know we sometimes eat the flesh of the sheep.

M. Yes, and God permits us to do this. He has given us a great many different kinds of beasts, and birds, and fishes, *for food.* And He makes the grain grow, that we may have bread; and all the different kinds of vegetables, and all the different kinds of fruit; - that we may eat them, and live; and be strong; and healthy; and be able to work; and be happy in doing good, and in loving and serving Him.

R. You forgot, mother, that God gives us the cow, too; so that we may have some of her sweet milk to drink.

M. I am glad you thought of it, Robert. *The pure clear water*, too, God gives us. How pleasant it is to drink it, when we are warm and thirsty. It is every where. If you dig down a little into the ground, you can find it. We want a great deal of water, every day. We want it, to wash ourselves and our clothes with; to cook with, and to drink. And God gives us a great deal of it. If we had not plenty of water, how much we should suffer!

R. Mother, *Oh! In how very many different ways God is good to us!*

M. Yes, Robert, we could as well try to count all the little sands on the bank of that river, to see how many there are, as to try to tell all the different ways, in which God is good to us.

R. Mother, there is one way, in which, I think, God is kind to *me*, but He is not kind to *you*.

M. What is that?

R. You have no kind father or mother to take care of you; but I have a mother, to take care of me. And I think God is very good to me, in giving me such a good mother. I love Him, and I love you, too, mother.

124

M. But, Robert, when I was little, like you, I had a kind mother, and father too, to take care of me. And now, you know, *God is my Heavenly Father*, and *He* will take better care of *me*, than *I* can of *you*.

R. Would God take care of me, if you should die? But I hope you will not, mother.

M. But I *must*, my son; and as I am a good deal older than you, I shall probably die before you do. If I do, God will take kind care of you, and will be *your Heavenly Father*, as indeed He now is. You must look up to Him for what you want, and think that *He will be better to you, even than I have been.*

R. I will try to do so, mother, but I shall be very sorry, indeed, when you die. I shall not see you any more.

M. Oh! Yes, my son, I hope I shall meet you again in Heaven, and that we shall see your father there, and that we shall all be happy together.

R. God is so good to us in this world, mother, that I am sure He will make us happy in Heaven.

M. He will, my son, if we love and obey Him. If we do not, we could not be happy, even if God should permit us to go to Heaven. But it is time for us to return.

So they walked down the hill, and went home.

QUESTIONS ON DIALOGUE VII.

What makes the bees happy?
If you are *idle*, will you be happy?
What did God make animals for?
What did God make the sheep for?
What has God given us for food?
Tell me *some animals or things* which God has given us, for our use and comfort.
Why is God very kind in giving us *water?*
Can you tell me in how many different ways God is good to us?
Who gave you kind *parents*, to take care of you?
Who gives you kind *friends?* Who gives you kind *teachers?* Who takes care of little children, when their parents die? Is God a very kind Heavenly Father *to you?*
Will He be your kind Heavenly Father, if you parents should die?
Will good people meet in Heaven?
Whom will God make happy in Heaven?
If you do not love and obey God, how would you feel in Heaven, if God should permit you to go there?

_____

_____

DIALOGUE VIII.

In the evening, after tea, Mrs. Stanhope took a short walk with Robert, in the garden. They walked there till the stars began to appear. The sky was full of them. And as the weather was very warm, Mrs. Stanhope was not afraid to sit down, a little while, in the evening air. So she and Robert seated themselves in the summer-house, and talked again about the goodness of God.

Mother. I am going to explain to you, my son, *some other ways*, in which God shows you, that He is very good.

Robert. I shall be very glad to have you tell me, mother.

M. God is very good to you, my son, in giving you everything which is necessary to keep you *in life* and *in health*, and to make you *comfortable*. But, besides all this, He gives you a great many things, to make you *more than comfortable*, to make you *enjoy a great deal*.

R. Oh! Yes, mother, how many pretty flowers God makes grow in our garden, for us to smell, and to look at!

M. Yes, Robert, and God has made thousands of beautiful flowers which *you* have never seen, and which *other people* are delighted to look at; and He has made the world full of beautiful things, so that, wherever we look, we may see

127

something to admire, and to show us, that *God wishes to make us happy.* Did you ever think, my son, why the grass is *green,* and not some other color?

R. No, mother, only I think, if it was *red,* and all the leaves on the trees were red, they would be so bright, that it would *hurt my eyes,* to look at them.

M. That is the very reason. No other color is so easy for our eyes to look at, a long time, as *green.* Have you not seen some persons wear *green* glasses?

R. I have, mother, but I do not know what it is for.

M. When they look through the green glasses, it makes *everything look green;* and as their eyes are sore and weak, and it hurts them to look at any bright things, the green glasses help their eyes very much.

R. How many curious things you know, mother. I wish you would tell me a good many more.

M. That I shall be glad to do, Robert. And the more you learn of curious things, the more you will see of the goodness of God.

He has made your eyes, not only *to see with,* so that you may walk about and not get hurt; but he has made them *to see thousands and millions of the beautiful things* which are all around you; so that you may have a great deal of pleasure in looking at them.

R. *Every time, mother, that I feel happy in looking at anything, I ought to think, how good God is to me!*

M. Yes, my son, and to thank Him for His goodness, and to feel, that you ought always to love and obey Him, if He is so good to you.

In the same way, Robert, think how many *pleasant sounds*, God has made for you to hear.

R. Mother, what do you like to hear best?

M. Some kinds of music, my son, but I hardly know which kind I like best. I am very fond of hearing the organ, and the people singing, at church.

R. So am I, mother; but there is one thing I like to hear better than that. I like to hear Aunt Mary sing a little song to me that I can understand. He sweet she sings!

M. How many sweet sounds there are for us to hear! God might have made our ears, so that we could only hear noises, and tell one thing from another; just as you know, when I speak to you, or, when Tray barks, or, when your kitten mews.

R. Well, mother, *I do not think we can ever stop finding out something about the goodness of God!*

M. If I had time, Robert, I could explain to you, how curiously God has made you body, and all the parts of it; so that it is a very convenient and pleasant body for your soul to be in.

R. I wish you would, mother, I want to learn all about it, and especially about the parts that are *inside*. Do you not remember, you told me something about them, when we were talking about the little wheels inside your watch that made the hands go?

M. I do; and I hope I shall be able, before a great while, to tell you about them. But when I do it, I wish to spend so much time in doing it, and to show you some pictures which I have, that you may be able to understand me well.

But I have one more thing to tell you, before we stop talking, to show you, how very, very good God is to you!

R. What is that, mother?

M. God has not only given you a very convenient and pleasant body for your soul to live in; but only think what a *strange and wonderful soul* He has made you, to live in this curious body, and *to use it, and to be good, and to do good, that you may be happy in this world, and happy forever!*

R. Mother, I use a good many things. I use my knife, and my bat, and my ball; but I do not exactly understand *how I use my body.*

M. You could not see, my son, or hear, or smell, or taste, or touch anything, *if your soul was not in your body.* When the soul is not in the body, the body is dead. And when the body is dead, the eye cannot see, the ear cannot hear, the nose cannot smell, the tongue cannot taste, the hand cannot touch.

R. Yes, mother; I remember it was so, when poor William Barker died. He could not move, or do anything at all.

M. And *you* could not move, or do anything at all, if your soul was not in your body. *It is your soul that sees with your eyes; and hears with your ears; and smells with your nose; and taste with your tongue; and touches with your hands.*

Why do you suppose I wear glasses sometimes?

R. So that you can see better.

M. Yes, and in the evening I could not see to read, at all, without them. They are like another pair of eyes to me. Now, when I take my glasses off, and put them in the case, *can they see, then?*

R. No, mother, it is not your glasses that see; it is *you that see*, through them.

M. Well, Robert, if my eyes could be taken out of my head, *they* could not see, any more than the glasses can in the case. And while my eyes are in my head, just as when my glasses are on, it is I *myself; the immaterial something inside of my body; the spirit; the soul; which sees things through, or with, my eyes.*

R. I never thought of that before, mother.

M. In the same way, Robert, it is *the soul that uses the body,* and the different parts of the body, to do a great many different things. Now think, how good God is, to give you such a curious and useful body, and then *to put in it such a strange and wonderful soul!*

R. Mother, do you think that my soul is a great deal more wonderful than my body?

M. I do, my son. And that is another reason, why you should love and obey God; because He has given you such a soul.

But we will talk more about this tomorrow. It is growing late, and the dew is beginning to fall a little. Let us go into the house now.

131

_____

QUESTIONS ON DIALOGUE VIII.

Who keeps you in life and health?
How does God keep you in life and health, and make you comfortable?
Does God give you anything to make you *more than comfortable?*
What does God give us the flowers for?
Has God made any flowers that *you* have never seen?
What did He make them for?
Tell me *some other things* which God has made, to give you pleasure, in looking at them?
Are there many beautiful things in the world?
Why do you think, that God wishes to make us happy?
Why is the grass green?
Suppose the grass, and all the leaves were *red?*
Why do people wear green glasses?
When you see curious things that somebody has made, what do you think?
When you see curious things that *live and grow,* what do you think?
Why did God make your eyes?
When you feel happy at looking at anything, what ought you *to think?* How ought you to *feel?*
What kind of sounds has God made for you to hear?
What do you like to hear best?
What *other sounds* do you like to hear?
Are *all sounds* pleasant to you to hear?
Could God have made you to hear only *noises,* so as to tell one thing from another?
Do you know all the different ways in which God is good?
Can you ever find them all out?
Who made your body? *What* lives in your body?
What *kind* of a body do you have?
Would you like to know about the many curious parts that are inside of your body?

132

What *kind of a soul* has God given you?

Why has God placed your soul in your body?

Does the body live after the soul has gone out of it?

When the body is dead can *the eye see?* Can *the ear hear?* Can *the nose smell?* Can *the tongue taste?* Can *the hand touch?*

What is it that sees with your *eyes?* That hears with your *ears?* That smells with your *nose?* That tastes with your *tongue?* That touches with your *hands?*

Why do people where glasses?

When the glasses are taken off, can the *glasses* see?

If my eyes were taken out of my head, could *they see?*

What is it, that sees through the glasses? *What is it,* that sees through my eyes? *What is it,* that uses the body, and its different parts, to do a great many things?

Which is the most wonderful, your *soul,* or your *body?*

How should you feel towards God, for giving you such a soul?

DIALOGUE IX.

The next morning, Mrs. Stanhope told Robert what God had commanded,--that we should *remember the Sabbath day, to keep it holy.*

She had explained this to him before, and he now thought of it a great deal; because he had learned so much, lately, about God, our Heavenly Father, who has given us the Sabbath, that we may have *one whole day* in the week to keep on learning more and more of His goodness; --to read *the Book* which He has given us; --to pray to Him, and to praise Him, both at home, and at the church;--to go to Sunday School; and to find out *how* we may love Him more, and serve Him better in doing good to others.

After breakfast, before they went to church, Mrs. Stanhope and Robert sat sometime in the *library*, and talked together.

Robert.   Mother, will you please, now, tell me something more about the goodness of God in giving me such a soul as I have?

Mother.   *Your soul, my son, is much more wonderful than your body.* Your body is matter, and will die, and crumble into dust. *Your soul is not matter.* It is immaterial. *It is spirit.* It will never die. *It will live forever.*

A wicked man might *kill your body*, and cut and break it into a thousand pieces. He cannot *do so to your soul.* He cannot touch your soul, to kill it, or to hurt it.

I can tie your body so tight, that you cannot move at all. I can keep you from using your body; from seeing, or hearing, or smelling, or tasting, or touching anything. But I cannot bind your soul. *No man can bind your soul, and keep you from thinking and feeling.*

R. Could not God, Mother.

M. Yes, my son, He made you, both soul and body. He preserves you, both soul and body. And if He chose, He could take away from your body all its life and strength, so that you could not use any part of it; and He could take away from your soul all its power of using your body; and all its power of thinking, and feeling, and acting. *He could make your soul die,* as well as your body.

R. Oh! How much more powerful God in than any man is!

M. Yes, my son, it was *His great power* that made your wonderful soul; and it is because He is *as good as He is powerful,* that He made your soul, so that it can keep on gaining more and more knowledge, and growing better and better, and becoming more and more happy, forever and ever, as long as God Himself lives; that is *throughout all eternity.*

R. Mother, I wish very much to learn how I must do all that.

M. My son, I am trying to teach you as fast as I can. One way is, to think what a wonderful soul God has given you. It is very different from that something inside of beasts which thinks and feels.

You cannot teach *them* anything about God, or what is right or wrong. How different you are from them, Robert. It is your kind, Heavenly Father who has made you to differ. Beasts do not know anything about Him, and therefore they cannot love Him. You know a great deal about Him, and *the more you learn about Him, the more and more you should love Him.*

R. You told me, mother, that my body has a great many curious parts inside of it. Has my soul parts, too?

M. No, my son. Remember your soul is *wholly unlike your body.* It is not matter. You cannot touch your soul. You cannot divide it. *It has no parts.*

Your soul does a great many different things, Robert. And when we wish to speak of the different things which it does, we have to use different words.

Sometimes you have one kind of feeling, and you say, *you are happy.*

Sometimes, you have a different kind of feeling, and you say, *you are unhappy.*

135

Sometimes, you love me, and are glad to do what I tell you to do, and I call you, *a good boy*.

Sometimes you have been obstinate, and have not done as I have told you to do, and I have called you *a naughty boy*.

Sometimes, you feel, as if you wished to make Eliza happy, and you try to make her so; and I tell you that is right and that you should always *be kind to her*.

One day she took your ball away, and ran off with it and you ran after her, and were going to strike her. You did not feel like being kind to her. You felt very differently, and I told you that it was very wrong for you *to be angry*.

Sometimes, you think what you did the day before, and can tell me all about it, and you say, *you remember it*.

Sometimes, you cannot think what a little boy's or girl's name is, and you say, *you forget it*.

Sometimes, after you have said your lesson, and I tell you that you may go and play, you think a little, and you feel as if you wished to draw your little wagon, and *you think all at once to go and do it*, and you say, *I will go*.

One day, Eliza asked you to go and build a little house for her. But you did not wish to. *You thought not to do it*, and you said, *I will not go*.

Now, when you are happy or sorry, good or naughty, kind or angry; when you remember, or forget, or will; it is *your soul feeling so, or thinking so, or acting so*. It is not *one part* of your soul which thinks, and *another part* which feels, and *another part* which acts. For your soul has no parts. It is one and the same soul which cannot be divided into parts; it is your *one, same self*, thinking, or feeling, or acting. Do you understand me?

R. I think I do, mother, pretty well. But, I suppose I can think, and feel, and act a great many other, different ways, besides those which you have told me about.

M. Yes, my son, and we have a great many *other, different names* to use when we talk about the soul thinking, and feeling, and acting in these other, different ways. But I shall have to tell you about them some other time. I have told you enough about them now, to lead you to think about how good God is, in giving you such a wonderful soul!

R. Yes, mother, and the more I keep on learning about it, the more I wonder. When I die and my soul goes out of my body, shall I think, and feel, and act as I do now?

M. I suppose you will think, and feel, and act very differently from what you do now, my son. But it is very difficult to think *how you will do it*. I cannot explain it to you. God, who made both your soul and body, and who put your soul into your body, knows how your soul, after it leaves your body, will live, and think, and feel, and act. He will give your soul power to do this. But He has not told us how He will give your soul this power.

But God has told us *in the Book which He has given us* that your soul will live after this body is dead; that it will live, and think, and feel, and act; that *it will live forever.*

If you love and obey God, and do what He has told you to do in His Book, *especially what He has told you about His Son Jesus Christ,* your soul will go to Heaven after your body is dead; and there you will see, and learn, and know, oh! I cannot tell you, how many good, and useful, and wonderful things. You will learn them easily and quickly. You will have a great many things explained to you which you *do not,* and which *you cannot* understand now. And you will keep on learning, and knowing, more and more of God, and of all the wonderful things which He has done and will be doing. In some way or other, *He will show Himself to you.*

R. Mother, *shall I see God?*

M. Yes, my son, if you go to Heaven, you will see your Heavenly Father. But *how* you will see Him, I cannot now think. I believe that you will because God Himself tells me so *in His Book.* And in Heaven you will not only be learning and knowing more and more; but you will not have any wrong thoughts or feelings, or wish to do any wrong things. You will be growing better and better all the while. You will have no pain, or aches, or sickness. You will never feel sorry. Nothing will give you any trouble. You will be very happy. You will be growing happier and happier all the while.

Everyone in Heaven, too, will be just like you, growing more wise, and good, and happy; loving and serving God more and more; and all loving each other, and seeking to make each other happy.

Sometimes when you have good things here, you think that they will not last long, and that makes you feel sorry. But in Heaven you will not feel so. You will know, and be sure, for God has promised it, that *all your good things will last, and will never be taken from you.*

Is not Heaven a very beautiful, and wonderful, and happy place? Is not God very good indeed to prepare such a place for you? Is He not very good to give you a soul which can learn about Him and about this beautiful place; and which can go there, and be happy with Him forever?

Oh! Think, my son, of this wonderful soul which your Heavenly Father has given you! Thank Him, for giving it to you and for all His other goodness towards you! Seek to know more of Him, and of what He wishes to have you do! Be careful not to displease Him! Love Him with all your heart! Learn to read, and to understand, the Book which he has given to you!

Remember, that before a great while, *you must certainly die!* Perhaps you may die soon! Get ready to die! Strive to get ready, when you do die, to go to Heaven! There you will see, and admire, and love, the goodness of God, forever!

———

Mrs. Stanhope and Robert now went out of the library, and got ready to go to church. Robert said nothing. But he thought, and he felt, a good deal. He thought of the wonderful goodness of God. He felt as if he wished very much to be a good boy, so that he might go to Heaven when he died.

———

QUESTIONS ON DIALOGUE IX.

Why has God given us the Sabbath?
Where does God tells us the purpose for the Sabbath?
What is your *body?* Will it die?
What is your *soul?* Will it die?
Can anybody *kill* your body? Can your body be *broken into parts?*
Can anybody kill or hurt your *soul?*
Can I keep your body from moving? Can I stop your seeing?
Your hearing? What else can I stop your doing?
Can I stop your thinking and feeling?
Could God destroy your soul?
Why do you think it was the great power of God that made your soul? Why do you think God was good in making your soul?
What do you think about the meaning of *eternity?*
How are you very different from the beasts?
Who made you differ from the beasts?
Why cannot beasts love God?
How should you feel about God, the more you learn about Him?
Has your soul parts?
Why do we use different words when we speak about the soul?
When do you feel happy? When do you feel unhappy?
When are you being a good boy? What are you being a naughty boy?

The Child's Book on the Soul

When are you kind to others? When are you angry with them?

When do you remember? When do you forget?

What do you say, when you think a little, and feel as if you wished to do something, and you think, all at once to do it?

What do you say, when you think, not to do a thing?

What is it within you that thinks, feels and acts?

Does *one part* of your soul think, and *another part* feel, and *another part* act?

Can the soul think, feel, and act a great many different ways?

Are there different *names* for all these different ways of the soul's thinking, feeling, and acting?

When your soul goes out of your body, will you think, feel, and act, as you do *now?*

Do you know *how* you will think, feel, and act when your soul goes out of your body? Do *I* know? *Who does* know?

How do you know your soul will live forever?

What must you do so that your soul may go to Heaven when your body dies? What will you do in Heaven?

If you go to Heaven, will you *see God?*

Why do you believe so?

How will you think, feel, and act in Heaven if you go there?

Is there anything in Heaven that can make people who go there unhappy? If not, why not?

Do people in Heaven learn much?

Do they become more good and happy?

How do they feel towards God and towards each other?

Will any good thing in Heaven ever be taken away?

What do you think of *Heaven?* What do you think of your *soul?*

What do you think of *God?* And of *the Book* He has given you?

When will you die?

What should you do to get ready to die?

———————
———————

DIALOGUE X.

After they came home from church, in the afternoon, Robert, who had been thinking a good deal all day about what his mother had been teaching him, asked her to go into the library and have some more conversation with him about *the goodness of God.* She said she would because he had behaved so well at church. And she took hold of his hand, and they went into the library, and sat down by the window, which was open, so that they could feel the cool breeze, and look out and see their beautiful garden.

Mother. I have told you, Robert, a great many different ways in which God is very good *to you.* But He is good *not to you only,* but to thousands and millions of other beings. He delights in doing good.

Robert. He has such great power, mother, that He can do a great deal of good.

M. Yes, my son, and *He is continually doing good.* Only think how many birds, and beasts, and fishes, and insects, He has made; and is all the while, taking care of; and giving them life, and food, and a great many things to make them happy.

R. But, mother, they are not as happy as we are.
M. That is true, my son, they are happy in a very different way from what we are. They are principally happy in

142

their bodies. We, too, can be happy in our bodies, but *we can be a great deal happier in our souls.*

They have, however, a good deal of enjoyment. And when we think how many millions and millions of them there are; almost all of them well and strong; and having enough to eat and drink; and bounding through the woods, and roaming among the flowers, and playing in the fields, and flying through the air, and sporting in the water; free from almost every care and trouble; and not afraid of death, because they do not know that they shall die; we may well think that they have a good deal of enjoyment; and we can see in them, how God delights in doing good.

But when we think of men, and women, and children, like ourselves, who have souls as we have, and who are able, as we are, to keep on learning, and able to become good and happy; when we think how many people there are now, and how many have lived in this world before us; and that God made them all, their bodies and their souls; and that He has taken care of them all; and that He wishes them all to be good and happy; and to live with Him, and be happy forever in Heaven; *how great, how wonderful, is His goodness!* We cannot think how great and how wonderful it is, any more than we can understand how great, and how wonderful God Himself is!

R. Mother, I think, I feel thankful to God for being so good to you and to Eliza.

M. And why, my son, do you feel thankful to God for being so good, *only to me and to Eliza?* Are you not glad that He is also good to your uncle John and to your aunt Mary; and to all the little boys and girls that you know; and to them too, that you do not know; and *to all the people in the world?*

Did God make the sun and moon and stars to give light *to you alone;* or the air for *you alone* to breathe; or other good things, to make *you alone* comfortable and happy? Other boys, and girls, and people, wish to be happy, as well as you or I. God loves them as well as he does you or me. He loves them *more*, if they are better than you or I. He made Heaven for others, as well for them, as for you or me. *You must learn to feel glad, that others are happy as well as yourself. You must learn how to make others happy, and so be like God.*

In Heaven all feel so, and all do so. Heaven is a world of love. If you do not learn to feel so, and to do so, you cannot go to Heaven.

R. Mother, I am afraid I have thought a great deal too much about how I might be happy myself, and a great deal too little, how I might make others so.

M.   Well, my son, I am glad that you begin to understand this. *You must strive to be like God, and do all you can, to make others happy.*

I wish you to be very attentive to me, now, while I tell you one other way in which God has been very kind to you.

R. I will, mother, what is it?

M. Do you see this Book? – (Mrs. Stanhope takes a Book from the table and lays it in her lap, and opens it.)

R. I do, mother.

M.   This Book we call *the Bible*. It is *the Book of God*, which He has given us; and in which He teaches us about Himself, and what He would have us to do, that we may be happy here, and happy forever.

R. Did God write it, mother?

M. He told several, very good men to write it. They wrote it a great many years ago. They wrote it at different times. Some wrote one part, and some, another. If God had not told them *what* to write, they would not have known what to write. He told them a great many things which nobody ever thought of before. He kept them from making any mistakes. He told them to write things about Himself, and about our souls, and about Heaven, and about Hell, which nobody could have ever found out, if God had not told those good men to write the Bible.

God has told us in the Bible all that is necessary for us to know, so that we may understand what *we must do* to avoid going to Hell, and to be prepared to go to Heaven when we die.

R. Oh! Mother, how good God is to give us the Bible!

M. Yes, my son. And the more you learn what is in it, the more you will know of God, and *of yourself*, too. And if you love the Bible, and do what it teaches you to do, you will find it *the best of all Books*. It will become very, very dear to you. It will seem to you, as it is, a *kind letter* from your Father who is in Heaven. He will seem to speak to you in every page. *He will seem to be near you;* to instruct you; to guide you; to advise you; to help you. If I should die, and all your friends and family should die; and you should be left alone, and be poor, and know not what to do, go to this Book, and believe that, in it, you will hear your Heavenly Father speaking to you. *He will be near you, to guide you, and to help you.*

And you must *ask* Him to guide, and to help you. *Tell Him all your troubles. Tell Him all your wants.* Feel truly sorry that you have ever done wrong. Tell God that you feel sorry. Ask Him to forgive you for your sins; and to teach you, and help you to feel right and to do right; and to keep you from feeling wrong and doing wrong. This is what we call praying to God.

145

Pray to Him, my son, daily. If you pray to Him *from your heart*, He has promised that He will hear your prayers, and do what is for your best. Pray in the words our Lord Jesus taught His disciples to pray:

> *Our Father which art in Heaven,*
> *Hallowed be Thy Name;*
> *Thy kingdom come;*
> *Thy will be done on earth as it is in Heaven.*
> *Give us this day our daily bread;*
> *And forgive us our debts as we forgive our debtors;*
> *And lead us not into temptation,*
> *But deliver us from evil.*
> *For Thine is the kingdom, and the power, and the glory.*
> *Forever. Amen.*

The bell now rang for tea, and Mrs. Stanhope and Robert ended their Sabbath afternoon conversation.

QUESTIONS ON DIALOGUE X.

Is God good to you *alone?*
Does He do a great deal of good?
Are beasts, and birds, and fishes, and insects happy in the same way that we are? Have they much enjoyment?
How do *they* show us that God delights in doing good?
How do *men, and women, and children* show us that God delights in doing good?
Can you understand how great the goodness of God is?
Do *you* wish to be happy? Do *others* wish to be happy?
Are you glad that God does good to *others?*
How must you learn to be like God?
How do all feel in Heaven?
How must *you* feel so that you may go to Heaven?

146

Have you thought much about how to make *others* happy?

Suppose your father and mother had always thought only how to make *themselves* happy?

What is the Bible?

What does God teach us in the Bible?

Did God write the Bible?

How did the men who wrote the Bible know what to write?

What would we have known about God, and our souls, and Heaven and Hell, if God had not given us the Bible?

If you love the Bible and obey it, how will it seems to you?

How can you seem to have God near you?

If you should have no friends, and know not what to do, *where* would you go to have God guide you and help you?

What should you ask God to do?

What should you tell God?

What is praying to God? Where do we learn *how* to pray to God?

What has God promised if you will pray to Him?

What is *the Lord's Prayer?*

How does this prayer teach us *how* to pray?

DIALOGUE XI.

Mrs. Stanhope and Robert rose early on Monday morning, and set out before sunrise to take a long walk. They went along the bank of a small river, not far from their house. It was the same river which they saw from the top of the hill where they sat down and had a long conversation, on Saturday morning, when Mrs. Stanhope said to Robert that they might as well try to count all the little sands on its bank, to see how many there were, as to try to tell all the different ways in which God is good to us. It was

147

a beautiful stream of clear water, and on one side of it, was a row of willow trees, in which the birds were singing. Now and then, a little fish would jump quite out of the water, and show his beautiful body of many bright colors. It was a fine morning, and Mrs. Stanhope and Robert thought once more of the goodness of God, in giving them so many pleasant things to make them happy, and they talked about Him, as they walked along.

Mother. Robert, I have taught you some things about God, which I hope you will remember, and which will do you good. I have told you a great deal of His love towards you, and towards others, and how much He has done to make you and them happy.

Robert. I thank you very much, my dear mother, for doing this, and I hope I shall never forget it.

M. Now, I have something more to tell you about God, which is very important for you to know. He is not only full of love and kindness, and delights in doing good, but remember also that *God is Holy.*

R. That is the word, mother, which I saw on the back of the Bible. It is called, *The Holy Bible.* What does the word *Holy* mean?

M. I will try to explain it to you. Suppose the Bible and a great many other books were lying on the table, in the midst of the library; and you and I were standing near it, and you did not know anything about the Bible.

You take it in your hands, and begin to turn over the pages, and to look at the pictures in it, and, pretty soon, to play with it.

I say to you, "Robert, you must not play with that Book. You may amuse yourself, and play with the other books if you do not hurt them; but you must *never* play with that book. It is *the Book of God,* which He has given us, to teach us about Himself. *It is very different from all other books in the world.* It is the very best of all books. You must not treat it as you do other books. You must not play with it, or laugh about it. When you take it, you must think what a good Book it is and that God speaks to you in it. When you read it, you should read it attentively, and seriously, and pray to God, to enable you to understand it. You should always think of it, and speak of it, and read it, and use it, in a very different way from what you do *all other books.*

The Bible is *God's Book. The Bible is a Holy Book."*

R. Mother, I hope I shall always remember this, and treat the Bible as a Holy Book. And I will tell sister Eliza to do so too.

M. In the same way, my son, we call a church, *a Holy place. It is the House of God,* where we go to learn about Him; to pray to Him; and to sing praises to Him. *A Church is very different from all other houses.* In other houses people eat, and drink, and sleep, and work, and buy, and sell things; but it is wrong to do so in the House of God. We should not play nor laugh there. We should be attentive and serious; and remember what we go there for; and think that God sees us, and that are in *His House.* It is very different from *all other houses. The Church is a Holy place.*

So God has commanded us to remember the Sabbath day, *to keep it Holy.*

It is God's Day, on which He has told us, we must not work, nor do as we do on other days. *It is very different from Monday, and Tuesday, and Wednesday, and Thursday, and Friday, and Saturday.*

We call them *week-days*. On those days you may play; but you should not play on the Sabbath. When the Sabbath comes, you should be quiet, and think much of God, and pray to Him, and read the Bible, and go to Church, and go to Sunday School, and try to learn more about God, and how you may love Him more, and serve Him better. The Sabbath is *God's Day*. It is very different from *the other Days. The Sabbath is Holy.*[1]

We call Heaven, to, *a Holy place*. It is that beautiful and happy place, where God and all good people live. *It is very different from all other places.* In other places there are pain, and trouble, and sorrow, and death, and wickedness; but in Heaven, there are none of these things. All there is pleasant, and bright, and cheerful, and happy. Everybody there is kind to everybody else. Each one tries to make all the others happy. Nobody there is wicked at all. Everybody is good. *There is no other place like Heaven. It is the place where God is. Heaven is a Holy Place.*

R. Oh! Mother, I wish I could see Heaven and all that is in it!

M. You *should* wish to go there, my son, because heaven is a *Holy Place*, and there is nothing wrong or wicked there. I hope you will indeed be a good boy, and love, obey and trust God, and then you will see Heaven, and all that is in it, and be good and happy there, forever.

Mrs. Stanhope and Robert were now returning, and very near their home. They soon ended their long and profitable walk, and went into the house.

---

[1] For a fuller discussion of this topic see the book *The Child's Book on the Sabbath* by Horace Hooker, republished by Solid Ground in 2006.

QUESTIONS ON DIALOGUE XI.

Is the Bible like other books? *Whose* book is the Bible?
What *kind* of book is the Bible? How should you *treat* the Bible?
How should you *read* the Bible?
Why do you call the Bible *holy?*
Is a church just like *other* houses? *Whose* house is the church?
What *kind* of house is the church?
What do people go to church *for?*
What do people do in *other* houses?
How should you *feel* and *behave* when you go to church?
Why do you call the church *holy?*
Is the Sabbath just like other days?
Whose day is the Sabbath?
What *kind* of day is the Sabbath?
What should you *do* on the Sabbath?
Why do you call the Sabbath *holy?*
Is Heaven like *other* places?
Who lives in Heaven?
What *kind* of place is Heaven?
Why do you call Heaven *holy?*
Why should you wish to go to Heaven?

DIALOGUE XII.

After Robert had said his lessons in the afternoon, and played
a little in the yard, he came to his mother and asked her to go

151

with him into the garden. Mrs. Stanhope consented. She walked in the garden, and picked some flowers, and Robert ran about for some time trying to catch his little rabbit, which had gotten out the box. He caught it at last; and then his mother and he took a seat in the summer house, and talked together once again.

Mother. Would you like to have me teach you something more about God, my son?

Robert. I would indeed, mother. But where have you learned all that you are teaching me about God?

M. *In the Bible,* my son. Do you not remember, I told you, that if God had not given us the Bible, we would have known very little about Him. *Almost everything that we know about God, we learn from the Bible.*

I told you this morning that the Bible is a Holy Book; that the church is a Holy Place; that the Sabbath is a Holy Day; and that Heaven is a Holy Place.

God, too, my son, is a *Holy Being. He is very, very different from all other beings.* He is different from them, especially in this, that *He is so good.*

Men, and women, and children have wicked thoughts. You know, Robert, that you sometimes think *how you will do something wrong.* You thought so, when you tried to open the lock the day that I shut you up in your room for being a naughty boy, and told you to sit still on the chair till I came and let you out. You had wrong thoughts when you tried to find some way to get up to the top of the shelf in the closet, after an orange which I put there, and told you not to touch it. Both these times you had wrong and disobedient thoughts towards me.

152

Some people have a great many wicked thoughts. They think about the bad things which they have done, and think of them with pleasure too. They think about bad things which they intend to do, and of the way in which they can do them. They do not try to get these thoughts out of their minds. They love to have them there.

But *God never had one wrong or wicked thought, or one wrong or wicked feeling.*

God has never said one wrong or wicked thing. All that He has told us in the Bible; all that He teaches us to think, to feel, and to do, is *like Himself,* good and right, as good and right as it can be.

God never did one wrong or wicked thing. Men do a great many things which they know to be wrong; and which makes them feel that they are wicked; and which makes them feel ashamed; and afraid of being punished. God never did so. He never did so, *ever so little.* He never thought, *ever so little,* of doing one wrong or wicked thing. He never wished, *ever so little,* to do so.

God is displeased with everything that is wrong or wicked. He dislikes it. He hates it. He cannot love you, when you have wrong or wicked thoughts, or feelings; or when you say bad words; or do wrong or wicked things.

God will forever keep every wrong and wicked thing out of Heaven. He is so good a Being; Heaven is so good a place; and all people there are so much like God, always thinking, and feeling, and saying, and doing, nothing but what is right and good; that He will always take care to let nothing wrong or wicked get into Heaven. For, if it should, it would make all the people there very unhappy.

You see, my son, how very, very good a Being God is. There *cannot be* anything wrong or wicked in Him; in what He thinks, or feels, or says, or does. *God is Holy. God is the Holiest of all Beings. GOD IS PERFECTLY HOLY!*

154

R. Mother, I am afraid I will never go to Heaven.

M. Why, my son?

R. Heaven is such a Holy place, and God is such a Holy Being, and *I am not holy.* I have had a great many wrong and wicked thoughts, and feelings; and I have said and done a great many wrong and wicked things. *I am still not holy,* and I am afraid I shall never be so.

M. My son, you must feel truly sorry, *in your heart,* that you have been wicked, and that you are still so. Tell God, *from your heart,* that you are sorry. Ask Him, every day, to forgive you, and to enable you not to have any more wrong or wicked thoughts or feelings; or to say or do any more wrong or wicked things. And *do you try yourself* to be a good boy, and to love and obey God, and to love and obey me.

If you do so, God will hear your prayers. He will help you, more and more, to be a good boy; and *to become holy;* and to get ready to go to Heaven.

R. But, mother, will God indeed forgive my wickedness, if I am truly sorry for it?

M. He has told us, my son, in the Bible, that if we repent of our sins, and believe in His Son Jesus Christ, He will forgive us, and that He will give us His Holy Spirit, to help us to do what is right, and to love and obey Him.

This Son of God came into our world, and here lived, and suffered, and died on the cross, that *through His sufferings and death* our sins might be forgiven, and that we might enjoy the love and favor of God forever.

R. Oh, what a kind Savior!

M. Yes, my son, and how kind God was, to give His Son to be such a Savior, and to send Him into the world that He might suffer and die for us!

How great will be our guilt, then, if we do not repent of our sins, and accept God's offers of mercy through Christ, and believe in this Savior, and love Him and do what He has told us to do.

R. Will you tell me, mother, more about this kind Savior, and what He has done for me?

M. Yes, I shall indeed be glad to do so. You know I have already, at different times, told you many different things about Him. But I will gladly tell you still more, and I hope, as you learn more and more of Him, you will love Him more, and serve Him better.

———

Mrs. Stanhope and Robert now left the garden and went into the house. Robert looked thoughtful and serious all that evening. He thought a great deal about getting ready to die, and go to Heaven. Before he went to bed, he prayed to God, alone in his room, as his mother advised him to do.

He hoped God would enable him to be a good boy. He remembered a good many ways, in which he had thought, and felt, and said, and done, what he ought not to. He determined that he would try to do so no more. He thought a great deal about God, and about His Son Jesus Christ, and of what his mother had told him he must believe and do, that he might have this Savior for *his Savior*. It seemed to him, as if he did indeed feel truly sorry for his sins and believe in Christ, and desire, above everything else, to love and serve God.

He began to think, that the Bible was indeed a wonderful and precious book. He thought, he would ask his mother to give him a Bible that he might have it *for his own;* and learn to read, and to understand: and that he might always keep near him, both when he was at home, or when he would go away anywhere, *this kind letter from his Heavenly Father.*

———

And why should not every little boy and girl feel and do as Robert? God invites them all to come to Christ. He invites you, my dear child, to come to Christ. Jesus Christ is ready, with open arms, to receive you to Himself.

Come to Him, and he will save you from sin and hell. He will take care of you most kindly and tenderly, while you live in this world. He will give you everything that He sees best for you. He will help you to *be good,* and to *do good.* He will be near you, to comfort and bless you, when you die, and then He will take you up to Heaven, there to be perfectly good and happy forever!

———

QUESTIONS ON DIALOGUE XII.

Where do we learn almost everything that we know of God?
What kind of being is God?
Why is God very different from all *other* beings?
Have you ever had wicked thoughts?
Have *other people* had wicked thoughts?
Has God ever had any wicked thoughts, or feelings?
Has God ever said or done anything wrong or wicked *ever so little at any time?*
Does God like anything that is wrong or wicked?

Can God *love you*, if you have wrong or wicked thoughts and feelings?

Can any wrong or wicked thing ever get into Heaven?

If anything wrong or wicked should get into Heaven, how would the people in Heaven feel?

Why do you say that *God is holy?*

Do you feel that *you* are holy and ready to go to Heaven?

How should you feel when you think you have been wicked?

What should you *tell* God?

What should you *ask* God to do?

What should you *try to do?*

If you do so, what will God do? How do you know for sure?

What *Good News* is there in the Bible, and what will the Bible tell you about it?

How should you *feel* and *act* towards God?

Who are *those* that God will never admit into Heaven?

Why should you *not* go with the wicked in this world, and *do as they do?*

Why did God send His Son Jesus Christ into the world?

Why did Jesus Christ have to suffer and die to save sinners?

Do you know and feel yourself to be a sinner?

Do you know what it means to believe and repent?

Do you ever think about getting ready to die?

Do you *pray to God?* What do you pray *for?*

Do you feel sorry that you have been wicked?

Do you determine that you will try to be good?

Do you wish to learn more about the Bible?

If you had a Bible of your own, what would you do with it?

If you *have* a Bible of your own, what are you doing with it?

Other Related Titles from Solid Ground

Solid Ground Christian Books is delighted to offer several books from Thomas H. Gallaudet and his friend Horace Hooker. The following books are in print and ready to ship.

THE CHILD'S BOOK ON THE FALL by Thomas H. Gallaudet is the sequel to *The Child's Book on the Soul.* It is an outstanding little book that introduces the significance of Genesis 3 at a level that can be understood by a child. This is a powerful book that will magnify the seriousness of sin and the glory of God's grace in the Gospel.

THE CHILD'S BOOK ON REPENTANCE by T.H. Gallaudet is a book that examines the specific area of repentance through the medium of dialogues between a mother and her three children. Once again this is a book that examines a critic issue in a way that can be understood by children. The author does an especially thorough job of exposing the danger of incomplete and false repentance.

THE CHILD'S BOOK ON THE SABBATH by Horace Hooker was one of Gallaudet's closest friends. He here lends his efforts to address an important matter in a most gracious and balanced way. Like his friend, Hooker uses the dialogues between a mother and her three children to address the various doctrinal and practical issues that surround the issue of the Christian view of the Sabbath.

OTHER RELATED BOOKS WE HOPE TO REPRINT...

THE YOUTH'S BOOK OF NATURAL THEOLOGY by Thomas Gallaudet is a book for children a bit older than the previous four titles we have published. In this volume the author again uses a series of dialogues and helpful pictures to lead the child to understand everything that can be learned about God from the world around us.

THE PRACTICAL SPELLING BOOK WITH READING LESSONS by T.H. Gallaudet and Horace Hooker
Two of the leading Christian educators of the first half of the 19th century joined their efforts to produce a remarkable tool for teaching both spelling and reading. This is a very rare volume that deserves a place in every home-school library, and in every Christian and public school. This will be useful even in teaching English as a second language.

Call us Toll Free at **1-866-789-7423**
Visit our web site at **www.solid-ground-books.com**

Other Solid Ground Titles

In addition to the volume which you hold in your hand, Solid Ground is honored to offer many other uncovered treasure, many for the first time in more than a century:

MARY BUNYAN: *A Tale of Persecution & Faith* by Sallie R. Ford

THE CHILD AT HOME by John S.C. Abbott

THE MOTHER AT HOME by John S.C. Abbott

THE FAMILY AT HOME by Gorham Abbott

SMALL TALKS ON BIG QUESTIONS by Selah Helms & Susan Kahler

OLD PATHS FOR LITTLE FEET by Carol Brandt

REPENTANCE & FAITH TO THE YOUNG by Charles Walker

THE KING'S HIGHWAY: *10 Commandments for the Young* by Richard Newton

HEROES OF THE REFORMATION by Richard Newton

HEROES OF THE EARLY CHURCH by Richard Newton

BIBLE PROMISES by Richard Newton

BIBLE WARNINGS by Richard Newton

BIBLE ANIMALS by Richard Newton

BIBLE JEWELS by Richard Newton

RAYS FROM THE SUN OF RIGHTEOUSNESS by Richard Newton

THE SAFE COMPASS AND HOW IT POINTS by Richard Newton

THE LIFE OF JESUS CHRIST FOR THE YOUNG by R. Newton

FEED MY LAMBS: *Lectures to Children on Vital Subjects* by John Todd

TRUTH MADE SIMPLE by John Todd

JESUS THE WAY by Edward P. Hammond

LECTURES ON THE BIBLE TO THE YOUNG by John Eadie

A MANUAL FOR THE YOUNG by Charles Bridges

ADDRESSES TO YOUNG MEN by Charles Baker

THE ASSURANCE OF FAITH by Louis Berkhof

THE SHORTER CATECHISM ILLUSTRATED by John Whitecross

THE CHURCH MEMBER'S GUIDE by John Angell James

THE SUNDAY SCHOOL TEACHER'S GUIDE by John A. James

DEVOTIONAL LIFE OF THE S.S. TEACHER by J.R. Miller

EARLY PIETY ILLUSTRATED by Gorham Abbott

Call for a complete Catalog at **205-443-0311**

Printed in the United States
97060LV00001B/148-156/A